THE CONVENTION AND THE CONSTITUTION

St. Martin's Series
in American Politics

EARL LATHAM

General Editor

THE CONVENTION AND THE CONSTITUTION

The Political Ideas of the Founding Fathers

DAVID G. SMITH
Swarthmore College

ST. MARTIN'S PRESS · NEW YORK

To Carl Brent Swisher—a student of the Constitution

Library of Congress Catalog Card Number: 65-15414
Designed by Jeanette Young
PRINTED IN THE UNITED STATES OF AMERICA
Second Printing

Preface

The object of this book is to examine the theories of government underlying the Constitution as it was originally framed. These theories were important to the Federal Convention of 1787 and in the Constitution drafted then. They are important, now, for students of American government, of political thought, and of American history.

The original Constitution has lasted, shaping our politics today. British constitutional historians, enjoying a more distant perspective of American society than we do, have commented that the American Constitution, not the British, is the great example of unbroken continuity. This appreciation argues the importance of looking to the original events and theories to understand the present American system. In this short book, I have given prominence to the larger questions of theory and constitutional strategy that are especially relevant for the United States today.

The Convention and the political ideas of the Founding Fathers are valuable also to the student of political theory. The delegates were thoughtful men, and many were acquainted with political history and with the intellectual heritage of their time. Because they were political leaders with an important practical aim, they often gave the ideas and theories of their time specific application that greatly illuminate them. For these reasons, the Convention debates are not only a part of American intellectual history but also of the larger Western tradition of constitutional and democratic theory. I have tried to show how the Founding Fathers built upon and enriched that tradition.

Many individuals have helped me in the writing of this book by their criticism, advice, and encouragement. I would like to thank especially Professor Charles E. Gilbert of Swarthmore College for his invaluable counsel and criticism, and Professor Frederick B. Tolles of Swarthmore College for reading parts of the manuscript, though I hasten to absolve them for any blunders I have committed. I should like also to acknowledge the expert and patient editorial guidance of Professor Earl Latham of Amherst College.

Contents

Chapter I

A BOLD DESIGN

The group of men gathered in Philadelphia in 1787 have been praised (or blamed) on several counts: for their boldness in launching the Constitution of the United States; for their effectiveness as politicians; and for their hardheaded prudence about government. The work of the Convention is also discussed in terms of "great compromises," and the Constitution itself has been called a "bundle of compromises."[1] These appraisals suggest that, in the main, the Founding Fathers ought to be congratulated for their skill at political manipulation.

The Federal Convention of 1787 was, however, a turning point in political history. Americans have regarded the Convention, naturally enough, as the beginning of their "great experiment" in federalism and republican self-government, the culmination of American attempts to meet practical domestic and international difficulties. But the Federal Convention was a larger event in its vision of government as a common human enterprise. It was a meeting of the eighteenth and nineteenth centuries. The American experiment continued an ancient political tradition—the aspirations for personal and corporate liberty and constitutionalism—but the Constitution was founded at the beginning of a new era

[1] Max Farrand, *The Framing of the Constitution of the United States* (New Haven: Yale University Press, 1913), p. 201.

that sought republican government, nationhood, and economic progress. The Federal Convention spanned the two eras and the Constitution itself was its bold design.

Despite the "bundle of compromises" theory, Americans pride themselves on the harmony of the Constitution's parts and the wisdom of the great design. Certainly, by the evidence of our own history, we must conclude that the Founding Fathers not only preserved a practical spirit of compromise but were lawgivers to a whole people. To achieve this aim, the Founding Fathers had to build upon basic principles and comprehensive philosophies of government. Yet they have seldom been judged for their philosophies of government. There is a coherent political theory of the Constitution. To understand the American system, we must also understand the political theory underlying the Constitution. The object of this book is to reconstruct that theory and examine it.

Law Givers

The delegates to the Convention understood their own importance in history. Though they worked with familiar institutions and received doctrine, their vision was, however, for a time when, as James Wilson said, "myriads of citizens . . . in future ages shall inhabit the vast uncultivated regions of the continent." Madison asserted—with perhaps excusable hyperbole—that their efforts would "settle forever the fate of republican government."

The delegates as practical men of affairs and experienced politicians shared a general awareness of the "magnitude of the object" and the enormous difficulties that lay ahead in moving toward national union and energetic government.[2] Madison, the most active of all the moving spirits for the new government, originally thought that the Convention would be a failure and urged Washington to use his influence to postpone it. The delegates said often and anxiously that the people at large understood little of their project. When they left Philadelphia in September 1787, though most of them were resolved to fight for adoption in their states and in the ratifying conventions, no one was entirely satisfied with the Constitution's provisions, and many expected that extensive amendments would be needed. Some felt that the Constitution would not be adopted, others that even if it were adopted it would fail to "carry its principles into the mass of the people."

Both history and philosophy suggested that the prospects for free government on a continental scale were bad. Experience argued that large territories and diverse peoples required either monarchy or imperial government. European experiments in free government did not offer hopeful precedents.

[2] Stanley Elkins and Eric McKitrick, "The Founding Fathers—Young Men of the Revolution," *Political Science Quarterly*, Vol. 76 (1961), pp. 181-218.

Under the British imperial system the colonists had lived with a kind of federal system: but a federal system that did not encourage a repetition of the experience. Absentee agents and officials who were ignorant of local conditions were among the evils that had driven the colonists to revolt. During the Revolution, the states had governed themselves independently and were not eager to subject themselves to a new government, especially one with substantial powers. In some states—Virginia and Massachusetts most notably—local patriotism was strong, and pride in the institutions of self-government was a thriving spirit running counter to national attachments.

The federalism of the Convention was of a new sort, envisioning laws that would act directly on the citizens through the federal courts and a national power of execution. But power is beneficent only if it is limited and directed. How were the delegates to achieve this end? As the North Carolina delegates wrote to their Governor Caswell, there seemed not "a single Straight or eligible Road that has been trodden by the feet of Nations . . ."[3] Abandoning the "sovereignty" of the states, what were they to put in its place? The politics of a federal system is at best complex. It requires uniting in one constitutional frame a working balance of power between the states and the central government and among the major sections of the country. It also requires supports and stimulus for a central political system. The absence of established political constituencies, national parties, and the social and economic bonds of union that attend modern society made the task of the delegates still more difficult.[4]

In establishing a republic the delegates were also breaking new ground. They drew, of course, on colonial and earlier British history. But many of the delegates also understood that a plan for independence and self-government, especially one intended for a whole nation, required them to go far beyond the experience of Europe and of their own colonial heritage. In the eighteenth century the concept of a constitution had been nurtured by monarchical government, by the struggles of kings and estates, aristocrats, provinces, town corporations, and the people. A constitution, according to the accepted liberal tradition was (ought to be) a contract between the people and the government—analagous to a legal instrument—in which the people delegated to the governors a

---

[3] Max Farrand, editor, *The Records of the Federal Convention of 1787* (New Haven: Yale University Press, 1923), Vol. III, p. 46. Hereafter cited as *Records*.

[4] "Federalism" as understood then was closer to what would now be called "confederation," a system in which the constituent governments bound themselves by compact, retained all or most of their sovereignty, and reserved control over local administration and execution of the laws. The federalism of the American Constitution was an innovation both because of the supremacy of the Union over many subjects of regulation and legislation, and because of grants of power for direct federal execution and administration.

restricted agency to secure and preserve a body of pre-existing rights. In the people existed the "original" of political power; they gave up a part of their rights to secure the rest.[5] Governments betrayed their agency and their trust, violating the original compact, when they invaded the reserved rights of the people or abandoned the original ends of government.[6]

The task of the delegates, however, was to move toward a self-governing republic, without a king and his monarchical establishment, without an aristocracy or a governing class. The *self-government* of a people required, therefore, more than the protection of its liberties. A free people must manage by its own political efforts to reconcile the authority of their own government with liberty for themselves severally and collectively.[7] They must, furthermore, create a corporate will among themselves to support constitutional change and growth.

To achieve a republic spread across a large territory, the delegates devised imaginative conceptions of self-government: the patriotic republicanism of James Madison, the "tory democracy" of Alexander Hamilton and Gouverneur Morris, James Wilson's ideal of a "popular pyramid."[8] They aimed at active and popular government on a "national" scale. The delegates knew as well the dangers that threatened from a "monarchy"; or in more contemporary language, a "dictatorship." They also feared "consolidation": an unchecked centralization of powers that would rob the federal system and the Constitution of vitality.

Consolidation or dissolution, dictatorship or anarchy, appeared to the delegates real enough possibilities. Some argued that the Constitution would itself fail, speeding one or another of these calamities. Others argued that only bold remedies could avoid them. But in all the deliberations one fact stands out clearly: the delegates' awareness of the weakness of the political supports upon which the national government was to rest. National leaders and republican virtue were in short supply. So

[5] John Locke, *Second Treatise of Government*, Ch. II.

[6] Cf. Thomas Jefferson, *The Declaration of Independence;* Carl L. Becker, *The Declaration of Independence—A Study in the History of Political Ideas* (New York: Vintage Books, 1958).

[7] John Jay, in a letter to a friend, stated the problem succinctly. The job, said he, is "to make sovereigns of subjects." Andrew C. McLaughlin, *The Confederation and the Constitution* (New York and London: Harper and Brothers Publishers, 1905), p. 42.

[8] The three approaches were the most important in the convention. "Tory democracy" was not the term used by either Hamilton or Morris but the term serves here to suggest the essence of their scheme: great authority in the central government and especially the executive, enabling the government to achieve popular support through vigorous action. By "popular pyramid," Wilson appears to have meant government broadly based in a democratic suffrage but moderated by the authority of its leaders and the public spirit of the citizenry rather than by the usual "republican remedies" (checks and balances, indirect elections). See Charles Page Smith, *James Wilson—Founding Father* (Chapel Hill: University of North Carolina Press, 1956), especially Chs. 15-17.

were political combinations and ties of sentiment and interest that transcended local or state boundaries. Thus, making the Constitution required also a plan for generating simultaneously the prerequisites of federalism and republican government.

The "magnitude of the object" naturally caused misgivings. As practical politicians the Convention delegates had to act boldly and energetically. But they had to do more than launch a new government. They were seeking also to give lasting vitality to a system of government, to establish a constitution that could "daily take on new powers." To achieve that aim they had to *plan*: to look to the future and to search for the lasting bases of government. They planned well. And they did so partly because they went beyond mere inarticulate premises to basic philosophies of government.

Modern America and the Spirit of the Laws

The contemporary world of nuclear deterrent and counterforce, automation, and civil rights demonstrations is far removed from the Philadelphia Convention. Since 1787, America has witnessed events little, if at all, anticipated by the constitutional authors: the emergence of a national party system; the egalitarian movements of the Jacksonian era; disruption and reconstitution of the Union; technological revolutions in industry, transportation, and communications; and, finally, the twentieth-century developments in foreign policy and international relations. As for the Constitution itself, fourteen amendments since the Bill of Rights have transformed that document, while many of the most significant phrases of the Constitution—"commerce among the states," "the general welfare," "necessary and proper"—have with time and through constitutional interpretation acquired new meaning patently contrary to the intent of their framers.

What value has a study of the philosophies of the Federal Convention for these times? Beyond the natural preference for a correct interpretation of the delegates' philosophies over an incorrect one, there are further considerations. Americans are among the most constitution-minded people in the world. They cast political quarrels in the form of controversy about the true and original nature of the Constitution or the intentions of Jefferson and Lincoln. In domestic and even international crises they invoke the historic origins and the original document. The old doctrines are used and abused in contemporary disputes over the separation of church and state, the rights of the states and the citizens in them, the constitutional role of the Congress, the President, and the Supreme Court. One purpose of the present inquiry is limited but essential: a defense against theories drawn from false premises about origins.

Inquiry into the original objectives and guiding philosophical principles of the Federal Convention also serves another purpose of greater intellectual importance. It contributes to an understanding of the basic principles of the American governmental system.

The scope of political change in America has been great and its pace rapid. American politics—as Alexis de Tocqueville observed in 1835 —exhibits an enormous agitation at the surface of events. There are also, he went on to say, deep continuities beneath the surface. Some relations do not change when others do, or they are recurrent, or they determine broadly the *patterns* that the changes follow. Even during the Revolution and the founding of the Constitution these continuities were evident: patterns of social mobility, trends of economic development, and distinctive methods of resolving political disputes.

The importance of these continuities to the underlying theories of government in the Federal Convention should be obvious. A stable and effective federalism rests upon and uses such continuities. Republican government lives and renews itself by serving and expressing lasting interests and enduring sentiments. Even the two conceptions of a constitution as a contract and a constitution designed for self-government are reconciled mainly by deep continuities of social and political life that in practice close the distance between the two conceptions. The Founding Fathers, in seeking to make a more perfect union and establish an energetic central government, had to discover the important continuities in American life and turn them to their own account. Their success is attested to principally by the unbroken and gradual evolution of American constitutional development.

The Founding Fathers were politicians and knew that the Constitution had to commend itself to a number of principal groups and sections.[9] But they wanted also a lasting frame of government, one that would capture the "genius of the American people." And when they moved from the task of finding the minimum that people would accept to "providing for our posterity,"[10] or securing for the future nation what was "essential to its happiness,"[11] they turned to first principles to establish a plan of government widely conceived. Thus, the underlying political theories of the Convention become important for understanding the American political system as a whole. Principles derived from such a study need, of course, to be taken provisionally. They should be checked against constitutional history, a knowledge of politics and government, and the more rigorous generalizations derived from political sociology. These principles, however, have an independent status that merits close attention. A constitution is to the political system as character is to a man. With constitutions, as with men, some of the original principles both influence and help to explain present behavior.

---

[9] John P. Roche, "The Founding Fathers: A Reform Caucus in Action," *The American Political Science Review,"* Vol. 55 (1961), pp. 799-816.

[10] As Roger Sherman said. *Records,* Vol. II, p. 3.

[11] Hamilton, *Records,* Vol. I, p. 283.

A Preview

Some years after the Federal Convention, and after Benjamin Franklin was dead, James McHenry, delegate to the Convention for Maryland, wrote in his *Anecdotes* recalling the events of those days:

> A lady asked Dr. Franklin Well Doctor what have we got a republic or a monarchy—a republic replied the Doctor if you can keep it.[12]

We do not know whether Franklin's rejoinder quieted the lady's fears, but several implications of his remark are clear. The Convention, without an army or a government at its disposal, without even the support of a broad popular mandate, could not *impose* a system of government upon the nation. The delegates could at most hope that their design for federal union and republican government would "meet with a response" and "extend an influence" into the consciences and political habits of the people. Franklin was commenting that no matter how grand the design, the Convention had only planned, hopefully begun, a continuing experiment in self-government. His remark also testified to a misgiving shared by many of the delegates: that the constitutional foundations might prove too weak for the great federal republic they had conceived.

The argument of this book accords with the tenor of Franklin's comment. The delegates met to consider a revision of the Articles of Confederation. From the Convention emerged a plan for a federal republic informed by an enlarged political vision and by generous principle. They acted boldly, in an almost revolutionary fashion. They also designed a new system, knowing that the political, the social, and the economic institutions of eighteenth-century America might prove inadequate to sustain the system. In short, they made a huge effort to give life to an ambitious scheme under relatively unfavorable conditions. We have already seen, in this chapter, that the delegates were aware of the difficulty of their task and that they realized a bold plan would be needed to accomplish it.

Chapter II examines briefly some of the unfavorable political and social characteristics of eighteenth century America. A vital concept for understanding the original Constitution and the Convention is that of the "disharmonious society." America was fortunately endowed and happily situated, yet it lacked many of the unifying and tempering influences that are important in the urban, prosperous welfare polities of the twentieth century. It particularly lacked constitutional and political supports for the new government.

The constitutional provisions that the delegates thought were needed to realize their vision are also the provisions most frequently criticized by succeeding generations for their antidemocratic spirit and tendency.

[12] *Records,* Vol. III, p. 85.

The issue between the Founding Fathers and their posterity covers both the question of the *motives* of the delegates and the *result* of their labors. Chapter III deals with the problem of intentions: with plausible and implausible interpretations of the motives and aims of the Founding Fathers. Many students of the Constitution and of the Convention itself have argued that the Founding Fathers intended principally to construct an undemocratic frame of government and to secure property and minority rights against popular excesses. A more plausible interpretation of the delegates' intentions was, simply, that they were seeking ways and means to connect a vision of a greater America with their present reality of an unstable polity lacking adequate constitutional supports.

Such an interpretation of the intention of the delegates also helps to explain the dualism between support for government and protections against governmental power that ran continually throughout all of the convention debates. To the minds of the delegates, political power above a local level was difficult to generate but absolutely necessary. That power was also dangerous, requiring effective constitutional restraints to check abuses. The provision for both constitutional powers and constitutional limitations depended upon devising extra-political institutions to carry a weight that the political process alone could not.

The dilemma of power against safeguards came to a crisis first on the issue of the federal system, and especially the "large state–small state" quarrel over the Virginia and New Jersey plans. There were, in fact, comprehensive theories of government underlying this quarrel that give considerably more political significance to the series of sectional compromises on the federal system. In Chapter IV, two separate philosophies —a nationalist theory and a strictly federalist one—are identified. These philosophies help to make clear the depth and significance of the factional differences over the federal system, as well as the intentions of the delegates in the constitutional devices that provided a basis for reconciliation between the two factions and their separate philosophies.

Convention debate over representation and the powers of central government also turned about the same central dilemma of power or protection. In arguing about the basis of representation, the powers of Congress, the relation of Congress to the President and of each to the political system, however, the principal philosophies were different from the nationalist-federalist division. The significant contrast was between moderate republicanism and monarchical principles. Chapter V argues that a unique synthesis of political philosophies gave a distinctive stamp to American institutions. Many of the latent properties of the American Constitution that we have subsequently recognized were at issue, not so much in the explicit provisions of the Constitution or the bare statements of the delegates, but in what the delegates understood those provisions and statements to signify.

The issues presented by federalism, and the organization of political will under the American system, emphasize the importance the delegates attributed to the role of law, to judicial institutions, and to the many devices in the Constitution designed to secure a "government of laws." Chapter VI explores yet another factional division and difference in philosophy: that between moderate republicans on the one hand and more radical federalists and republicans on the other. The debates in the Convention explain much of the importance assigned to law and judicial methods as part of the ordinary processes of American government and politics.

The American Constitution was a remarkable synthesis of eighteenth-century political philosophies, probably the greatest representation of the political thought of that period. The Constitution was also the work of men who looked ahead to a transformed society and economy and prepared for the crises that would arise in later generations. Chapter VII, the concluding chapter, puts the question: how well does the original plan continue to serve?

Chapter II

SOCIAL AND POLITICAL ENVIRONMENT

The task that the delegates faced in 1787 was to build a new system upon old and generally accepted foundations. For generations they had been English subjects; now they were American citizens. They had fought a revolutionary war; and then they had experienced a decade of self-government. Yet they still lived with social, legal, and political institutions descended from England.

The war for independence was primarily a national revolution—an assertion of freedom from foreign rule—rather than an internal or domestic revolution. Loyalists and former ruling groups were in some cases driven out and their property confiscated after the war. During the Revolution, the individual rights of the common man were given wider recognition through bills of right and amendments of the common law with respect to entail and inheritance, quit-rents,[1] and master-and-servant relations. The suffrage was expanded, though not rapidly, in several

[1] *Entail:* restrictions upon the transfer of landed property, especially through wills. *Quit-rents:* money payment in lieu of feudal or semifeudal servitudes.

states, and in all states the legislatures assumed a new importance, gaining power at the expense of the executive and the courts. Some have argued that the Revolution enthroned democracy and that the Convention was a counter-revolution by the national "establishment." But the two periods did not differ so much. The war of independence did little more than accelerate internal social and political trends long evident in colonial society.[2] Moreover, in many areas there was little democratic progress at all: social relations remained unchanged, and local oligarchs entrenched themselves on the withdrawal of English authority.

The Revolution removed the restraining grip of Britain in two important areas: the external controls of the Crown in commerce and foreign policy were eliminated, and so were the agents of British authority within the states—the governor and his council, the courts, military and civil officers, and many of the established families. The colonists found themselves free from "unconstitutional" taxes and domestic interference, but they also lost some of their former advantages and protections. In particular, they lost British protection from foreign powers, assured markets, and the advantages of stable, constituted domestic authority. For some this situation was all to the good. Others found it wanting; and if they did not hanker for a restoration of imperial authority, at least wished for some compromise between the old and the new. All faced the problem of what self-government ought to be.

Under the Articles, the colonies had prospered and languished, cooperated and quarreled. Though some states and some groups were hard pressed, it was not a time of general misery. Still, many collective interests made themselves felt, and there was much talk of constitutional revision or further amendment of the Articles to strengthen them, to promote commerce among the states, or provide for an adjudication of collective and individual disputes.

Many wanted different governmental arrangements: revised state constitutions and a new government above the former colonies. As to the second of these concerns, the people and the states disputed what that government should be, how powerful it should be, and what should be its spirit or temper. The philosophy of the delegates now becomes important. For what kind of society was the Constitution designed; and what were its intents and objectives? A partial answer to the first of these questions is that the Constitution was designed for an eighteenth-century society. What is important about that description is the subject of this chapter.

---

[2] J. Franklin Jameson, *The American Revolution Considered as a Social Movement* (Princeton: Princeton University Press, 1926); Frederick B. Tolles, "The American Revolution Considered as a Social Movement: A Re-evaluation," *American Historical Review*, Vol. 55 (1954), pp. 1-12; Oscar T. Barck, Jr., and Hugh T. Lefler, *Colonial America* (New York: The Macmillan Company, 1958), Chs. 32, 37.

Political Systems

In the seventeenth century, the colonies were politically diverse. Royal colonies, proprietary colonies, and charter colonies varied widely in their laws and political institutions. During the eighteenth century, the colonies grew more alike—in social structure, political institutions, and governmental practices—until they were rough copies of British government.

As in Britain, local autonomy was the rule. Cities and counties, though legal creatures of the state, acted for themselves through their mayors and county officers and justices of the peace. Local government was subject to the review of the central courts, the governor and his council, and finally the Privy Council and the Board of Trade in England. But that supervision on the whole rested lightly, for it was mainly a power of veto and judicial review rather than one of administrative direction. Colonies and their local governments responded to local needs and pursued their own aims for years with no significant hindrance from English authority.

The common law, which served in place of much administrative regulation and statute law, and also provided for the arbitration of personal and group claims, was regarded by the colonists as their inheritance. They claimed the liberties protected by the common law, and followed as well many of the substantive provisions of English law so far as they answered to local conditions of land tenure, contract and tort, commercial dealings, and master-and-servant relations; but they moderated the authoritarian tendencies of eighteenth-century English jurisprudence, especially in respect to criminal law and public order. The colonists were students of Coke rather than Mansfield; indeed, when they read Mansfield or Blackstone they often ignored the authoritarian precepts that English judges had drawn from the same materials.[3] As an instrument of social control and political agency, the common law played a role similar to its function in England. But as the colonists "received" the common law they adapted it, bending it to the local conditions and the ends of their own society.

By 1760 the structure of central government was roughly the same in all the colonies, except that in two charter colonies, Connecticut and Rhode Island, the governor was elected. Appointed governors, assisted by their councils and the assemblies, exercised powers in the colonies like those of the king of England. As in England, the executive quarreled with the assembly over "prerogative," over appointments, salaries and revenues,

---

[3] Sir Edward Coke, a seventeenth-century English jurist, defended the common law and Parliament against the prerogative of the king. The first Earl of Mansfield (1705-93) was known for his authoritarian jurisprudence and for advocating a policy of coercion toward the colonies. Blackstone's *Commentaries on the Laws of England* were widely studied in the states, as was Coke's *Institutes*.

and the control of courts and administration. But in the more egalitarian society of America, executive authority and the surrogates for the crown fared worse than the king in England, at least until 1760. From England came continual "Instructions," exhortations, and regulations designed to tighten the imperial controls and preserve the prerogatives and interests of the crown. Despite the prestige of the office, the power of appointment and veto, the support of the central courts, and a council representing the notables and aristocrats of colonial society, the governors lost ground throughout the eighteenth century.[4]

A common superior government over the states was provided by a system of imperial organization designed to advance England's foreign trade, to protect her colonial interests in North America, and to secure harmonious principles of government throughout the colonies. This imperial organization was the parent, or perhaps the stepfather, of American federalism. The system, terminating in the Board of Trade, the Privy Council, and the Crown, secured to the colonies common external defense and a central management of their collective interests. The American remembers mainly the Navigation Acts, the taxation to support British agents and military personnel in North America, and the invasions of local and personal liberties by writs of assistance, the quartering of troops, and riot acts. Imperial organization, however, protected the colonies in foreign affairs and international trade, provided an army and navy and fortified borders, established a currency and trade regulations, and stood as a court of last instance to resolve disputes arising between the states and, occasionally, between individuals and groups within a state. The system, laxly and incompetently administered, usually by absentee agents, was ultimately directed to the interests of London merchants. In *form*, however, the imperial system resembled closely the federal system that finally superseded the two Continental Congresses and the Articles of Confederation.[5]

Two political facts stand out in the period after the Revolution. One is that the new states carried farther the political tendencies apparent under colonial government. Weak executives, separation of powers, and the dominance of the legislative characterized the new state institutions, as did short elective terms, recall of delegates, and an expanded suffrage. By the 1780's a counter tendency was in evidence, and, in several states, executive councils were replaced by popularly elected governors who had substantial powers of veto or revision, second houses were added, and legislative terms lengthened.

---

[4] On the government of the colonies, see Barck and Lefler, *op. cit.*, Ch. 15; Leonard W. Labaree, *Royal Government in America* (New Haven: Yale University Press, 1930; Curtis P. Nettels, *The Roots of American Civilization* (New York: F. S. Crofts and Company, 1946), Chs. 7, 20.

[5] Andrew C. McLaughlin, *A Constitutional History of the United States* (New York: D. Appleton-Century Company, Inc., 1935), Chs. 2, 3.

A second significant fact was the vanishing of a common system of external control provided by the British. The Articles purported to put some system in place of the former imperial organization. Yet the colonists wanted to have their cake and eat it too. The Congress of the Articles was enjoined to act like a government, but it lacked the authority and resources to do so.[6] Gone were many of the features of imperial control that Americans had found galling, but so were the coercive powers of the common government. Under the dual impact of an assertion of local sovereignty and the disappearance of an external system of control, postrevolutionary politics developed strongly centrifugal tendencies. Interest in trade and the fear of external enemies sometimes worked for unity; but often they worked for dissension. Not surprisingly, a dominant theme in the Convention was the economic, military, and political advantages of union. Union was considered especially necessary in a world of mature European powers and a system of international trade that required collective power to improve the terms of trade for the Americans. Equally troublesome to the Founding Fathers were state legislation and policy that fostered dissension between the states. America is "beheld with jealousy," wrote John Jay to Gouverneur Morris; and "jealousy is seldom idle."[7]

The Economy

The economy of the United States, at the time of the Revolution and the Convention, was not yet one of extensive markets, many commercial or industrial enterprises, or vigorous competition—that is, it was not the economy of laissez-faire capitalism celebrated in Adam Smith's *Wealth of Nations*. The principal occupation was agriculture, carried on, for much of the population, on a subsistence basis. In other sectors of the economy—manufactures, commerce, and the supply of credit—units were small, often involving no more than one individual trading on his own account, a master and an apprentice manufacturing for a limited market, occasionally a merchant or manufacturer with wealth enough to be called a capitalist. Markets were local and restricted in scope by primitive transportation and local monopolies. Large-scale enterprises, usually of a commercial sort, were sometimes undertaken by joint venture. But generally they were difficult to get under way, in part because neither market conditions nor the technology of the period encouraged them. The absence of organized banking or widespread use

---

[6] See opposite page.

[7] Quoted in Charles Warren, *The Making of the Constitution* (Boston: Little, Brown and Company, 1928), p. 13.

MAJOR PROVISIONS OF THE ARTICLES OF CONFEDERATION AND PERPETUAL UNION

The States

1. Bound themselves together in a league of friendship, mutual support, and honor.
2. Were prohibited from: maintaining standing armies; making war (except in case of invasion) or entering into treaties with another state or a foreign power; levying any impost or duty interfering with the treaties of the United States.
3. Were enjoined to: accord free passage, the privileges of trade and commerce, and the privileges and immunities of free citizens in the several states to inhabitants of each state; render up fugitives from justice; to accord full faith and credit to the "records, acts, and judicial proceedings" of other states.

The Congress

1. Was appointed annually "in such manner as the legislatures of each state shall direct," and its delegates were subject to recall.
2. Could provide for the exercise of an executive power (in fact exercised through committees of the Congress).
3. Had power: to make peace and war and enter into treaties and alliances; to equip an army and navy, requisitioning the states for money, supplies, and men; to borrow money, emit bills of credit, and pledge the credit of the United States; to appoint the superior officers of the United States Army; to provide for the arbitration of boundary and land disputes between states; to provide for a postal system; and to regulate trade with the Indians.

In essence, the Articles ratified the form of government that had grown up during the war for independence. It was weak government, partly because union is a slow process, whatever the form of government. The central government was also given few powers and could exercise only those that were expressly delegated. Most notable among the disabilities were:

1. Congress lacked the power to tax or to regulate commerce.
2. No provisions were made for enforcing the decisions of the Congress either by sanctions applied to the states or their officers or through laws operating directly upon individual citizens.
3. There was no system of federal courts (except for a Court of Appeals for Admiralty, established in 1780).
4. Congress, when acting with respect to war, commerce, foreign relations, money or requisitions, could act only with the assent of nine states.
5. Amendment required unanimous consent of all the states.

of the corporate form of economic organization further restricted collective economic effort.

The economy tended to be "mercantilist" or monopolistic.[8] People needed and expected local government to intervene on their behalf and to use the police power to benefit the "community." The community was benefited by the restraint of a nuisance or the dedication of an inn or mill to public use. Benefits also took the form of exacting tolls to support a local enterprise or securing a favorable trading position for local merchants against outsiders. Often, too, local power was used to relieve the economically distressed by staying the execution of mortgages and bills of credit. Direct regulation by local and state government supplemented and controlled the economy and remedied in some measure the poverty of collective resources. The same regulation also raised the issue of the exploitation of government for private ends and the monopolization of advantages by established individuals and groups that had arrived early on the local scene. Towns often dealt unfairly with local farmers to the advantage of town merchants. They provided bounties and subsidies that to those outside the protected circle seemed a robbery of the public treasury. Eastern territories, which served as distribution centers and sources of credit for those in the west, exacted levies and tolls and sought to preserve and exploit their favorable position. States responded to economic fluctuations or adverse balances of payments and to local mercantile and producer interests by passing laws favoring now merchants and shipping interests, at another time the debtor or primary producer. The society was one of cheap land and westward movement, of new opportunity; it was also one of many local monopolies and devisions between the entrenched and the newer arrival.

If the term "corporate economy" can be used to describe America today, America of 1787 might be characterized as a "contract" economy. The country lacked money and credit, large economic organizations, and an advanced productive technology. People relied partly upon contractual relations as a substitute. Productive organization depended upon agreements between master and servant, and larger undertakings contracted out many operations. Promoters borrowed to speculate in lands and lent in turn to farmers to make their speculations going concerns. Eastern merchants who served as intermediaries for foreign and domestic trade were the capitalists upon whom depended inland commission merchants. Contract substituted in considerable measure both for capital and for or-

---

[8] The term "mercantilist" is here used to signify only some of the practices of earlier European mercantilism, particularly interference with the domestic economy by regulation of industry and commerce, granting subsidies, and establishing monopolies or economic privileges designed to stimulate the economy.

ganization. To us, today, bank notes, shares of stock, and the corporate board are familiar legal forms of economic activity. The eighteenth century knew primarily contract, the law of agency, mortgage and assignment. These devices were the instruments which made possible economic activity beyond the local area and agrarian employments; they were the building materials of economic progress.

These two aspects of the American economy—the mercantilist and the contractual—were complementary in some ways and antagonistic in others. A government operating on mercantilist principles supplemented what individuals could do for themselves. Bounties and monopolies provided incentives to act and offered security against a turn of the market unfavorable to entrepreneurs. Similarly, local regulations controlling trade or protecting one link in a chain of contracts could contribute to the prosperity of many local enterprises and even the whole local economy. But one group's interest is often another's loss, particularly in the arms-length world of contractual relations. The mercantilist tendencies of local and state governments also imperiled economic progress, especially the contractual superstructure upon which nonagricultural and nonlocal enterprise depended.

During and prior to the Convention, opposing factions agitated fiercely, on one side for paper money and bills of credit, on another side for the protection of sound money and contract. The issue was an important one. Securing the obligation of contract and providing for hard currency often benefited mechanics and merchants at the expense of debtors, especially farmers. Strong protections for contract and sound money also limited the principle of local mercantilism and the liberty of each community to arrange economic matters for itself. But these same protections were, given the contractual aspect of the economy, the conditions for commercial and industrial progress and the foundations for economic unity—for an economy that could function effectively above the local level.

The Society

The Americans of the eighteenth century had much in common with each other, particularly in origin, political culture, and aspirations. They were overwhelmingly Protestant and tended toward congregationalist and democratic views of ecclesiastical authority. They were English or North European, with only a sprinkling of other stocks. In the main outlines of political culture, there was substantial agreement: most wanted a constitutional republic with a large measure of local autonomy and freedom for the exercise of individual initiative and industry. Social mobility, local "boosterism," emulation, and striving for material betterment were characteristic of American society then as now.[9]

But a persistent theme of group conflict underlay American politics and society in the eighteenth century. The horizontal cleavage of rich and poor, aristocrat and commoner, was less important than in Europe,[10] but vertical lines of division were plentiful.[11] Sectional cleavages followed lines of settlement, lines of economic development, and the paths of rivers and mountains. They existed not only between Easterner and Westerner, the North and the South, but within each state or region. Sometimes cultural and religious differences reinforced other divisions. The Revolution also left behind its residue of group animosities. Other "sources of faction" especially important to the Convention were the vertical lines of division between town and country, creditor and debtor, importer and producer, merchant, professional, and planter.

The attitudes of exclusiveness and competition that accompany new settlement and continuing migration also affected America in the eighteenth century, as they do now. The new arrival demanded a place in his adopted society. Established families, and even those who themselves had arrived only a decade past, were determined to protect their identity by excluding the presumptuous immigrant.

Furthermore, the colonies had been governed separately by England, and had dealt individually with the Privy Council and colonial administration. Although political practices tended to converge on a common model, the colonies lived apart. Around each state government developed well-established political interests and loyalties that reinforced other differences in social habit or sentiment.

The primitive communications and the local orientation of much of trade and industry emphasized local interests. At the same time, the influences and institutions working for unity above a local level were few and weak. Only a few groups transcended state lines: military officers, merchants, and a few politicians of national outlook and national experience. Parties tended to be assemblages following a local notable or loosely organized cliques; they failed effectively to link communities either in political association or in action on issues. They lacked the "machinery to polarize, mobilize, or stabilize public opinion . . . ,"[12] especially in politics above the local level. Few pluralistic social checks or organized political agencies moderated social, economic, or political conflict in

[9] Cf. Curtis P. Nettels, *op. cit.,* Chs. 17, 18.

[10] Cf. Louis Hartz, *The Liberal Tradition in America* (New York: Harcourt, Brace and Company, 1955).

[11] Robert E. Brown, *Charles Beard and the American Constitution* (Princeton: Princeton University Press, 1956), pp. 30 ff.

[12] William N. Chambers, *Political Parties in a New Nation—The American Experience, 1776-1809* (New York: Oxford University Press, 1963), p. 23.

American society. Such was the situation and the problem as the Founding Fathers in the Convention saw it.

A final point needs to be made concerning the political potentialities of the "disharmonious society." Such a society, if it is self-governing, tends toward expanding political conflict. It does so because government is weak, and because other social and economic influences do not moderate the collision of conflicting interests and sentiments. An example typical of the political situation in many local communities and states of eighteenth-century America illustrates the pertinence of this argument for the present discussion.

The local community is a mixed economy: partially agrarian but depending upon credit and the market also. "Old family" creditors (perhaps Tories) established in business, the local government, the churches and social circles, secure and exploit their position by local ordinance and control of the courts. The opposition are recent arrivals, more numerous, of a different religion, smarting from a bad turn of the market or a harsh execution of the laws. Political competition is relatively free and open so that political organizations and the press can take sides and give vent to their sentiments. They have little sense of political restraint nor any great respect for the truth. Though the powers of local government are limited, either side can change the rules by appealing to a superior government—to amend the suffrage, the property laws, or the powers of government itself. Each does so through agitation and "conventions," petitioning direct relief in the form of stay laws and force bills, new remedies for execution, and so forth. The consequence will be a lively politics. The result may also be expanding political conflict that will not only set citizen against citizen but also destroy government and constitutionalism itself.[13]

Expanding political conflict results from three properties of eighteenth-century society. One is the presence of cleavages or conflicts of interest that reinforce each other: as when new settlers are set against the established old families. Second, there is both opportunity and incentive to use government itself as a weapon in group conflict: to secure a monopoly or protect entrenched political position. These alone tend to produce intense political conflict. Add the fact that the rules of the game are uncertain and especially that partisans can and will, given the opportunity, change them to their advantage, by either capturing the local political machine or invoking the force of a superior government. Such a situation tempts one faction to do unto others before others do unto

---

[13] A good description of group conflict can be found in Jackson Turner Main, *The Antifederalists—Critics of the Constitution, 1781-1788* (Chapel Hill: University of North Carolina Press, 1961), pp. 40 ff.

it. It supports the strategy of warfare, and not of peaceful political competition.

A decisive item in considering the Convention and the Constitution is that there were many influences working for unity and for common prosperity. There was also the possibility of an expanding political conflict.

Chapter III

THE FRAMERS' INTENTIONS

This chapter has two objects. One is an inquiry into the intentions of the Founding Fathers, necessary because of the enormous controversy over their original purposes. But the same inquiry also establishes the historical and theoretical perspectives needed to understand the original constitution itself.

The Controversy Over Motives

Early controversies over the Constitution, especially those engaged in by antebellum political leaders, appear to have been over what the Constitution ought to say or mean. When Madison and Jefferson drafted the Virginia and Kentucky Resolutions (1799) to protest broad interpretations of national power, or when John C. Calhoun wrote his *Exposition of 1828* to defend state sovereignty, they looked to basic constitutional theory rather than to an alleged intention or motivation of the Founding Fathers. The quarrel over motives first arose after the Civil War. The generation that followed the Compromise of 1877[1] faced many new social and economic problems attendant upon rapid industrial de-

[1] The Compromise followed the disputed Hayes-Tilden presidential election and resulted in an end to Reconstruction policies and a number of agreements between economic interests of the North and the South.

velopment and population movements, and it searched anew for the fundamentals of American politics. Out of this era came a spirit of "constitution worship" and an interpretation of the Federal Convention termed by one historian the "chaos and patriots to the rescue" theme.[2]

John Fiske, a historian widely influential at the turn of the century, was one of the leading worshippers. The title of Fiske's book—*The Critical Period in American History, 1783–1789*—suggests his point of view.[3] For him, the period under the Articles of Confederation was a time of economic chaos, depression, and group and local struggles that were rapidly moving the thirteen states toward anarchy and dissolution, if not civil war. The convention delegates were patriots distressed at the fate of their country, seeking to ward off either anarchy or dictatorship. The Constitution they made necessarily curbed liberty and confined democracy, but they established a sturdy republican frame of government—conservative though it may have been—that proved itself immune to the worst diseases of popular government. Is not the lesson clear? At least by implication? The Constitution is the salvation of the country. Learn its principles and abide by them, no matter how attractive mass democracy or sharing-the-wealth may for the moment seem to be.

Constitution-worship was profaned early in the twentieth century by a generation led by the historians Charles Beard and J. Allen Smith.[4] According to Beard, who wrote the most controversial interpretation of the Convention, the Constitution was not the fruition of Anglo-Saxon liberty; still less was it an impartial judicial instrument protecting the good of all. Behind "justice" and "the Constitution," Beard saw groups of men and economic interest, even a hint of conspiracy. The Constitution, he said, was not the creation of disinterested patriots, nor did it represent the will of the whole people. The men who drafted the Constitution had personal pecuniary interests. The adoption of the Constitution also was originated and accomplished principally by "four groups of personalty interests which had been adversely affected under the Articles of Confederation: money, public securities, manufactures, trad-

---

[2] Merrill Jensen, *The New Nation—A History of the United States During the Confederation—1781-1789* (New York: Alfred A. Knopf, 1950), p. xiii.

[3] New York: Houghton, Mifflin Co., 1888.

[4] Of course other influential works on the Convention appeared during this period. Some were important in shaping later views: for example, Max Farrand, *The Framing of the Constitution of the United States* (New Haven: Yale University Press, 1913); and Andrew C. McLaughlin, *The Confederation and the Constitution* (New York and London: Harper and Brothers Publishers, 1905). Farrand described the Constitution as a "bundle of compromises" achieved by practical men with practical and immediate aims. McLaughlin argued that the Constitution was the natural culmination of colonial experience. The views of these men were influential, but did not disturb anyone. The theses of Beard and Smith, however, have upset a good many people since the early 1900's. They also produced one of the "great issues" of American historiography that has continued to this day. For this reason, the ensuing discussion deals principally with their arguments.

ing and shipping."[5] J. Allen Smith had earlier drawn a conclusion that Beard might well have endorsed: "In the United States at the present time we are trying to make an undemocratic Constitution the vehicle of democratic rule."[6]

Whether right or wrong, Beard's interpretation of the Convention has been enormously influential. It shocked some and comforted others of the Wilsonian era, and was almost received doctrine during the New Deal.[7] Historians and political scientists have continued to this day to reinterpret the Convention and to quarrel with Beard and his spiritual kinsmen.[8]

The alleged economic motivations or antidemocratic intent of the Founding Fathers, even if the allegations are true, do not rob the Constitution of legitimacy nor destroy the importance of the political theory underlying it. For whatever the intent, the result stands independently. The dispute over original intentions has, however, directed attention away from the larger principles of the Constitution to an inconclusive debate over the interests, motives, and group loyalties of the Founding Fathers. For this reason, alternate interpretations of the delegates' motives, or different ways of looking at the same facts are important to an understanding of the Constitution itself.

Beard argued that the motivation of the Founding Fathers and of the supporters of the Constitution was principally economic. Yet the men who made the Constitution, and many who were active—either for or against ratification—had also serious political motivations. Without denying that economics may have been important, the political motives of the delegates must be included to establish the context within which they acted. In some instances the latter motives were, properly, separable from the economic, and in some instances they were directed toward larger and more inclusive objectives than the economic ones.

Smith, Parrington, and others have stressed the antidemocratic intent of the delegates and compared the Convention and the adoption to a counter-revolution. But they paid little attention to the society for which the Constitution was made. In fact, the political objectives of the delegates were sensible ones, given the society in which they lived.[9]

---

[5] Charles A. Beard, *An Economic Interpretation of the Constitution* (New York: Macmillan, 1913), "Conclusion," especially pp. 324-325.

[6] J. Allen Smith, *The Spirit of American Government* (New York: Macmillan, 1907), p. 31.

[7] One author states that 37 of 42 new college texts adopted Beard's interpretation in 1937. Robert E. Brown, *Charles Beard and the American Constitution* (Princeton: Princeton University Press, 1956), p. 9.

[8] See, for example: Lee Benson, *Turner and Beard—American Historical Writing Reconsidered* (Glencoe, Ill.: The Free Press, 1960); Forrest McDonald, *We the People—The Economic Origins of the Constitution* (Chicago: Chicago University Press, 1958); John P. Roche, "The Founding Fathers: A Reform Caucus in Action," *The American Political Science Review*, Vol. 55 (1961), pp. 799-816.

[9] The argument to be made with respect to this point depends upon Chapter II.

According to the interpretation suggested in this chapter, the delegates were attempting *in the main* to create a political system and not to protect property. They were also attempting *principally* not to defeat democracy but to devise strong constitutional and political supports for a federal republic. They had a large and generous vision of the future. They also understood the limitations of their constitutional and political resources. They sought to connect their ambitious vision of the future with their present political world.

The Founding Fathers: Accused and Defended

The indictment by Beard, Smith, and Parrington includes three counts. One is that making and adopting the Constitution was an act of usurpation. Another is that the Constitution was designed largely to protect property interests, especially personalty or property other than land. The last count is that the Constitution was antidemocratic both in design and in substance. We shall deal with each of these charges, but first, an elaboration of the indictment as a whole.

A bill of particulars can be made, with no great difficulty, that the delegates acted without authorization, that they usurped power, and that they acted on their own account. Following the Annapolis Convention of 1786,[10] Congress had passed a cautiously worded resolution calling upon the states to send delegates for the "sole and express purpose of revising the Articles . . . ," and providing that any amendments required the approval of Congress and of all the state legislatures.[11] Under these instructions, delegates from twelve states convened in Philadelphia. No one would dispute that they went beyond their mandate; and indeed, most of them apparently intended to do so even before they met as an assembled convention. In Convention, with organization and procedure settled and a secrecy rule adopted, they passed the first of the Randolph Resolutions: "That a National Government ought to be established consisting of a supreme Legislature, Executive, and Judiciary."[12] With no more ado, the Articles were discarded, so far at least as the activities of the Convention were concerned. The Convention also violated the provisions of the Articles by stipulating that the Constitution be ratified by approval of conventions in nine of the states. We can argue, as did the delegates, that a "higher trust" bade them strike boldly and carry the Constitution to the "people."[13] Yet there was a taint of usurpation in their action.

---

[10] Convened to consider commerce along the Potomac. The resolution appears to have been the work primarily of Hamilton, and was the most important act of the Convention.

[11] A proviso that would seem reasonable given the authority under which the Convention was to meet and the explicit provisions of the Articles.

[12] Warren, *op. cit.*, p. 146; *Records*, Vol. I, p. 30. Notice the use of the word "National." It does not appear in the final draft.

[13] Warren, *op. cit.*, p. 346; *Records*, Vol. I, pp. 122, 123.

The delegates constituted a small, cohesive elite, perhaps one of the most powerful and tightly knit groups of men that have acted upon the American national scene. They were financially and professionally successful: merchants, planters, bankers and lawyers. They were knit together by ties of family and acquaintance, and by years of service in national activities—in the army, the Congress, and the diplomacy and administration of the peacetime years. They were also men of great political influence: former and present governors, leaders in national administration, and representatives in Congress. The company has often been cited for its talent and intellectual ornaments. It is equally noteworthy for the collective influence it could and did wield. If we say that the Convention usurped power, we ought to add that from the nature of the company and their political relations they were in a good position to make a constitution inimical to the real interests or desires of the people.

The delegates did not subscribe to that complex of values today associated with liberal democracy. They openly declared their hostility to democracy as a method of government, to popular state legislatures, and to the democratic provisions of the Articles. They were concerned particularly to withdraw the power of decision from the "grass roots" and to strengthen the less directly representative branches of government. They attempted as well to *fragment* the public will by such devices as separation of powers, the independence of the judiciary, diverse representation and "filtration,"[14] and separating the states into politically "isolated compartments." By the interpretation of many of their own radical contemporaries, they were undoing the Revolution and preparing the ground for a future aristocracy.[15]

Finally, a principal object of the Constitution was, simply and plainly, to restrain the states in order to protect property. The Constitution, Beard pointed out, can be largely described as a creation of central authority to protect and advance property interests through the four great powers of taxation, war, commercial control, and the disposition of western lands, and as an instrument designed to withhold from the states a power to menace property: the ban on paper money and the protection of contract.[16] Furthermore, personalty was given a distinct preference, despite the overwhelmingly rural and agrarian character of the country.

The Founding Fathers were not, by the standards of their time, democrats. They acted to protect property and to restrain the states. They used their influence to make a constitution "over the heads" of the local assemblies, the states, and the Congress of the Articles. From this recital

---

[14] "Refinement" of political opinion by indirect election.

[15] See Jackson Turner Main, *The Antifederalists—Critics of the Constitution, 1781-1788* (Chapel Hill: University of North Carolina Press, 1961).

[16] Charles A. Beard, *op. cit.*, pp. 176-178; Forrest McDonald, *op. cit.*, p. 9.

alone, Beard's principal contention of an overriding economic motivation is persuasive. So, too, is the charge of Smith and Parrington that the delegates undemocratically made an undemocratic constitution.

Defense: An Alternate Interpretation

The bill of particulars given above is, so far as it goes, true. The main issue with Beard, Smith, Parrington and other idol-smashers, however, is the interpretation of the acts of the delegates. Interpretation depends upon context; and an alternate interpretation depends upon enlarging the context within which the delegates acted. That enlarged context is the "disharmonious society" for which the Constitution was made. That context does not destroy the anti-Convention indictment. It simply demonstrates that the indictment can be subsumed as incidental to a bigger purpose: to erect a large political edifice upon weak constitutional foundations.

We return briefly to the eighteenth-century society described in the preceding chapter. The society was disharmonious because it tended toward group and sectional particularism, and because the political attitudes needed to support common republican government were not firmly set nor strongly entrenched. There were few of the moderating influences that we associate with democracy in modern, urban, and industrialized societies: intersectional ties, a national economy, and a wide sharing and communication of common political attitudes. Eighteenth century society, furthermore, lacked many of the institutional resources with which to create a "reasonable" or "moderate" politics, to borrow the language of that time. Parties were loose factional assemblages; and political communication was poorly organized. Under all these circumstances, and despite all that worked in favor of republican government, the danger of expanding or "cumulative" political conflict was a very real, if not always present, threat.

The language of the delegates in Convention supports a view that they were primarily concerned with creating a constitution for a "disharmonious society" lacking adequate supports for a moderate federal republic. Their speeches and their language do not support an interpretation that they wanted primarily to defeat democracy or erect an anti-popular oligarchy. In the florid oratory of the opening days of the Convention the delegates denounced the democratic provisions of the Articles and of the state constitutions, the rage for paper money, and the unreasonableness of the people. But for the most part, they spoke of different fears: of cabal and faction; of dissolution or consolidation; of monarchy or popular upheaval. They were fearful mainly not of democracy or attacks upon property, but of continuing, unchecked tendencies to an extreme, and of political expressions that would undermine republican government itself.

The constitution the delegates constructed indicates also that, whatever may have been their other concerns, they were fundamentally engaged in an attempt to strengthen the American polity so that the future republican government could function effectively. Their strategy—logical under the circumstances—included three principal methods or aims. One was to withdraw especially fruitful sources of contention from the most quarrelsome and heated centers of political dispute and thereby limit a tendency toward cumulative political conflict. Another technique of the delegates was to strengthen both the political and nonpolitical bonds of unity. And lastly, also in keeping with rational strategy under prevalent political conditions, they sought to create an artificial frame of government to limit and to sublimate the natural tendencies of politics in their "disharmonious society."

The delegates withdrew power from the states; especially they withdrew some principal objects of political contention from the reach of local democracy. The Constitution prohibited interference with contracts or with commerce among the states. It also enjoined each state to grant "full faith and credit" to the public acts, records, and judicial proceedings of other states and to recognize for the citizens of each state the "privileges and immunities" of citizens in the several states.

By one account, in these provisions the delegates acted to limit democracy and to protect property. By another, they attempted to remove sources of contention from the power of the states, to provide for a national citizenship and for a new government with power to act as representative and trustee of citizens possessed of a dual citizenship.

Actually, the delegates in Convention seemed to be relatively indifferent to the *internal* politics of the states. They did not consistently take the side of debtors or creditors, democrats or oligarchs. Nor did they appear to fear local democracy as such. They did not care, either, how many heads were broken on the local level. But they were intensely and continuously concerned with political conflict that weakened the union, undermined a growing nationhood, or threatened the stability of a republican government.

Aside from the provisions cited and those designed to secure national control of foreign relations, the states were left substantially in charge of their own affairs. They retained their traditional police power almost in its entirety, along with control over property, crime, civil injuries, and social arrangements. The delegates removed from the states very little. Indeed, to have done so would have, in their view, both threatened to create a monarchy, centralized discontent, and made the common government itself too much subject to contention. Instead, they sought to create an additional tier of government and a new constituency principally to defend and represent what citizens enjoyed in common as Americans.

Those objects of political controversy that the delegates sought to protect from the states were critical in amending the major defects of their disharmonious society. A national commerce and protection of common rights would contribute both to a national citizenship and to removing causes of dissension among the states. Their protection would encourage both political and economic growth. And by putting them out of the reach of the states and local governments, some of the heat would be removed from a politics that tended dangerously toward cumulative and uncontrollable conflict.

Aside from an attempt to withdraw certain subjects of contention from state action, the delegates were also especially concerned to strengthen the bonds of union. The contract and commerce clauses, indeed all of those clauses of the Constitution that deal with property, need to be read in this context. The delegates set up protections for property, for commerce, and for sound money. They particularly sought to protect the foundations upon which personalty and economic endeavor rested. To follow the delegates in Convention is revealing. They discuss property, the commerce clause, and conflicts of debtors and creditors. But they talked directly about these matters very little. They are discussed almost wholly in conjunction with *other* objects: navigation acts, the slave trade, the burden of taxation, etc.

Property found its place among many other interests, and especially as an adjunct to *political* objectives such as military strength and corporate unity, or *social* objectives such as access to unappropriated resources and equality of status. Usually, the delegates seemed primarily interested in settling upon one or another social or political objective. The battles in the Convention about these interests or ends were often fierce. When agreement was reached, economic arrangements appeared to follow pretty much as a matter of course and even of indifference. Often they were simply taken over from some clause in the Articles, or from a practice made familiar by their colonial experience. One may say, then, that economic and property arrangements were subordinate to the interests of federal union, political stability, and the future economic and social development within the United States. The delegates adopted those property arrangements they felt would conduce the long-term interests of the nation they saw growing from their efforts.

Property was protected; and a measure of control over property and especially personalty was withdrawn from the states. The delegates may have incidentally benefited the interests of creditors or merchants or speculators. In fact, they did not seem specifically to want to protect them. In any case, they had other ends. One was withdrawing a source of controversy from direct political action by the states. The delegates were also filling out and giving specific character to a conception of national citizenship and of future national development. And they were, finally, artificially strengthening the polity by associating union and common republican government with economic advantage and development.

The delegates' treatment of democracy, or popular government, probably appears by contemporary standards the most suspect of all their deeds. Notice again, however, that an interpretation of their actions depends upon the context in which they are read. Their actions could have been aimed at weakening democracy. They could also have been intended to strengthen artificially a republican government under circumstances requiring precisely that approach to secure a popular government on a national scale. The delegates sought to erect a national government. They sought to establish a dual citizenship under which people would be at once members of a locale and of a state, but would share in a joint venture of federal and republican government. They created scope for an additional layer or level of government, an independent government with its own machinery of courts, its own taxing powers, and a capacity to develop loyalties. They knew the tendencies of the politics of their time. Consequently, they sought equally to guard against the most dangerous tendencies of the government they were creating.

The Founding Fathers called themselves supporters of republican government, by which they meant representative government, derived from the great bulk of the people, but so arranged as to secure stability and government of the wise and virtuous. They meant by "wise and virtuous" primarily wise in the ways of politics and filled with republican virtue. The delegates understood from their own experience that the government, to work at all, required political leaders at the national level with considerable disinterested devotion to the republic. Remember their experience: their enormous efforts and great difficulty in getting the project started and their many frustrations. They had seen how readily jealousies could set individuals and sections against each other. From their experience—under colonial governments, during the Revolution, under the Articles—they knew that a stratum of patriots was not only a necessary support to government, but a needed security against factionalism, cabal, or disruptive parochialism.

A prime objective of the Convention was, therefore, to provide for moderate and independent leadership for the nation in spite of the masses or popular majorities, especially those within the states. The delegates feared also a plebiscitary chief on the national scene or a widespread populistic democracy. Against these dangers, they devised a set of "republican remedies" to apply to the federal government itself. Their "republican remedies" had another purpose: to complete and perfect the representative republic itself.

The representative devices in the Constitution serve both to temper political will and to supplement and complete it by providing representation for interests that might otherwise remain unheard. Representation in the Constitution was the subject of sectional and factional compromise. These compromises had also (and were understood to have) a broad tendency to supplement and expand political representation. In sum, the representative arrangements in the Constitution, whatever other purposes they had, were also designed to offset the defects of political representation that arose from an inadequately organized politics.

Today, we are apt to think of checks and balances, separation of powers, and indirect representation as devices to restrain the "tyranny of the majority," and to thwart popular government. In part they have that effect. But in the eighteenth century, they were good republican and democratic devices and, in fact, applied consistently and rigorously by radical republicans in the states. When commending such devices in the Convention, the delegates sometimes spoke of the danger of majorities or omnipotent legislatures. A more central concern was cabal and faction: the threats of silent and sinister accumulations of power and of the disruption of the polity by minority interests. The delegates were trying to generate a national will, not defeat it. A central danger, as they saw it, was that such a will would not be representative, that it would be a will proclaiming itself the representative of the whole but masking designs for power, pelf, and preferment. Separation of powers, checks and balances, and representative formulae would work to counteract the natural tendencies of politics built on a primitive economic and social base. Such devices were also vital for nourishing the government itself: to secure confidence in it; to win the support of disinterested patriots; and to afford a security against fecund evils.

A democrat might say that the delegates took too low a view of politics. Perhaps they did. But that judgment misses one of the unique and original contributions of the Founding Fathers. They contrived an alternate and supplementary system of institutions to remedy the deficiencies of their own political society. The delegates' constitutional methods of fragmentation, of withdrawal and delegation, and of nourishing a patriot elite are directed to this object. They wished to stimulate loyalty to the principles of republican government. They wanted also to generate power in the whole system. They sought to achieve both these ends by limiting politics—that is, politics in the ordinary sense of the word. But in constraining and narrowing the method of politics, they supplemented the Constitution, providing for alternate methods, other modes for the resolution of conflict, and for stimulating patriotic energies.

Eighteenth-century philosophers often spoke of a social contract and of a political contract or contract of government. These terms are useful in the present context. The task for the delegates was to build a nationwide political contract upon an untried and possibly inadequate foundation. For this purpose, they required more than a simple principal-agent model of government. Neither the existing society nor contemporary political institutions could sustain a republican government based upon a direct connection between political will and government response. Supporting the political contract required artful measures. Consequently, the delegates contrived methods to strengthen particular political institutions by formal constitutional provisions and to sublimate intense political passions by utilizing the forces of social and economic evolution. American politics was "judicialized." Many issues that involved property, citizenship, and the development of the nation were reserved from the direct or speedy expression of popular will. Even ordinary political decision was closely associated with the politics of federalism and an intricate constitutional system of representation and separation of powers. According to one view of democracy, the delegates dethroned the people and set up an antidemocratic scheme of government. But "politics" in the narrow usage of that term is a small part of the whole of the life of man, and even a small part of what most understand democracy to be. Whether the delegates' conception of the right relation between citizens, the society, and the state, between the social contract and the contract of government, was an ungenerous one or even an antipopular one, remains to be discussed in later chapters. Certainly we can say, however, that their conception was statesmanlike.

Conclusion

The intention of the delegates probably cannot be finally known. But if we establish a purpose that included a wider intention and motive than that imputed by Beard or Smith, we lay a foundation for the ensuing discussion. Without alleging proof, it would be useful to state what seems the most plausible interpretation of the delegates' intentions.

In the context of their society and their experience with the colonial and revolutionary governments, the delegates' activities in behalf of the new government seem to have been directed primarily at a simple, coherent set of *political* objectives. They seem to have been aiming at (1) withdrawing particular objects of contention from local majorities; (2) attempting to secure a common interest; (3) securing the support for the "representative republic" of a stratum of "wise and virtuous" leaders who would put republican principles above personal and factional interest; and (4) devising a scheme of representation and checks and balances that would complete that government and prevent it in turn from developing cumulative tendencies toward an extreme.

The delegates, in Convention and out of it, appear to have been doing what people have generally thought they were. They protected property, but especially in order to remove sources of discord, foster economic growth, and develop interest in the government. They destroyed the dependence of the government upon the states, but more in the interests of a national citizenship than fear of democracy. Similarly, they added to central government the "salutary checks" of republican government as much to complete a representative will as to restrain it. In Convention and out of it they did not act as if they were trying to execute a *coup* for their faction, defend property, or silence democrats in the states. They were men engaged in a task intellectually and practically of enormous difficulty: to conceive a successful constitution and launch a nation. That task required great initiative and sound principles of strategy and philosophy.

The difficulty of the task answers at least partly the charge of usurpation. Without any doubt the delegates violated their mandate. They also appealed from the Congress and the states to the ratifying conventions. While their deeds lacked constituted political legitimacy, that same defect also puts a different face upon their actions. The Convention was not a government. The delegates could at most hope to persuade the active electorate, assuming that elections to the conventions would be held. Against their cause they had two of the most powerful of political influences: inertia and fear of the unknown. Under the circumstances, the charge of usurpation does not seem a grave one.

Beard and Smith remind us that the Founding Fathers lived long ago and that they made a Constitution to serve, initially, a society of a few million farmers. There is no security that their philosophy will continue to serve us, especially at times when new popular creeds are struggling for recognition. To their credit, however, the Founding Fathers did not finally settle the issue between republican government and responsiveness to popular creeds or democratic majorities. Instead, they initiated a dialogue between the people as ultimate sovereign and the people as *populus,* as trustee for the nation.

THE FEDERAL CONVENTION 1787

May 14–24	Preliminary meetings
May 25–28	Organization
May 29	Proposal of Randolph (Virginia) Plan and Pinckney Plan
May 30–June 11	Debate on the Randolph Plan, ending in adoption of its main provisions
June 15	The Paterson (New Jersey) Plan; revolt of the "small state" delegations
June 15–30	Two weeks of debate over the two plans
June 30	The Compromise Committee is appointed
July 5	Report of the Compromise Committee proposing popular representation in the lower house, equal representation in the upper, and origin of all money bills in the lower house
July 5–16	Debate on the Connecticut Compromise
July 16	The Compromise is adopted
July 17	Agree to a judicial negative of unconstitutional state acts
July 23	Adopt the provision for per capita voting in the Senate
July 26	Agree upon a single executive: a President to be chosen for a term of seven years and ineligible for re-election
August 8–10	Agreement upon qualifications of voters and representatives and upon the regulation of elections.
August 15–23	Debate on the powers of Congress (Article I, Sections 8 and 9)
August 24–25	Debate on the powers of the President
August 28	Adopt restrictions upon the states
August 29	The "three-fifths" clause; the slave trade; and the commerce clause
August 30	Agree upon the provisions for admission of new states
September 6	Agree to election of the President by electors in the states and with no restrictions upon re-election
September 7–8	Agree upon the annexation of the Senate in the appointive power and in the treaty-making power
September 10	Provision for amendments to the Constitution
September 12	Report of the Committee of Style
September 17	Signing of the Constitution and Adjournment

RATIFICATION

Delaware	Thirty members ratified unanimously December 7, 1787
Pennsylvania	Ratified by a vote of 46 to 23, December 12, 1787
New Jersey	Thirty-nine delegates ratified unanimously December 18, 1787

Georgia	Twenty-six delegates ratified unanimously January 2, 1788
Connecticut	Ratified by a vote of 128 to 40 on January 9, 1788
Massachusetts	Ratified by a vote of 186 to 168, February 16, 1788
Maryland	Ratified by a vote of 63 to 11, April 26, 1788
South Carolina	Ratified by a vote of 149 to 73, May 23, 1788
New Hampshire	Ratified by a vote of 57 to 47, June 21, 1788
Virginia	Ratified by a vote of 89 to 79, June 25, 1788
New York	Ratified by a vote of 30 to 27, July 26, 1788
Rhode Island	Ratified by a vote of 34 to 22, May 29, 1790
North Carolina	Rejected, 193 to 75, August 4, 1788; finally ratified November 21, 1789

Chapter IV

FEDERALISM

The Federal Constitution is woven of consistent threads of philosophy and political aim. Many of its principles and aims stand out most clearly, however, if we view it as a fusion of two political systems: republican government in the ordinary sense of the words, and a federal state. The delegates saw the need for a republican government that would be proof against faction and cabal or the ambition of a great man. Federal government, a "more perfect union" was equally important, and was in fact the occasion for the Convention itself. In pursuit of this latter object, the delegates were occupied with strategies of union, resolving sectional conflict, and protecting local interests. They were engaged with the sectional politics of a diverse "empire" united by ties that might prove strong if they were wisely knit, but that would prove fragile if subjected to the haphazard strains of group and sectional conflict.

Along with sectional bargains and specific constitutional prohibitions intended to protect the interests of states and regions, two general philosophies of union are important in American federalism as initially planned by the delegates. One aimed at close union and a common national citizenship; the other at a loose, decentralized association of relatively autonomous parts. The latter is termed here "federalist."[1] The two

[1] The terms "nationalist" and "federalist" as used here agree with the usage of the time of the Convention. A "nationalist" advocated not only a powerful union, but one achieved through the surrender of a considerable measure of state "sover-

philosophies—"nationalist" and "federalist"—were expressed particularly in the Virginia and New Jersey Plans respectively. They were also articulate philosophies that remained crucial throughout the whole of the Convention and figured in many provisions touching upon the federal system. The federal provisions of the Constitution and the philosophies underlying them are especially important in understanding the specific quality, the "spirit" of American federalism and in interpreting the sectional bargains designed to supply the ties of union.

Two Plans and the Connecticut Compromise

The Convention began with a decisive and brilliant victory for the principle of nationalism. That victory was also a personal triumph for those with a national vision—especially Madison, Hamilton, Charles Pinckney, and James Wilson. It was no less a triumph for Washington and Robert Morris, who had acted, rather than written and planned systematically, and who were less theorists than men of solid practical vision and aim.

On the first day of debate, the Randolph Resolutions, more familiarly known as the "Virginia Plan," were introduced, followed by a similar scheme, Mr. Charles Pinckney's "Plan."[2] The Virginia Plan, the main subject of discussion during the opening weeks of the Convention, was a program for a strong union and a vigorous central government resting upon the people. Most probably the work primarily of James Madison, it expressed the Madisonian vision of a union capable of directly enforcing equal and national laws. For most of the "nationalist" faction in the Convention, it was a maximum plan, their "Utopia."[3]

For a time, the scheme appeared to be near adoption. The Convention agreed to discard the Articles. They agreed to two houses of the legislature and a popular election of the lower house. They accepted the proposal of a strong executive. They moved steadily onward to adopt a provision for a national veto of state laws and for a national judiciary that could enforce federal laws directly upon the citizens. Within two weeks the delegates had canvassed all the main subjects and substantially

---

eignty." The "federalist" wanted the states to retain their sovereignty substantially intact. In later controversy over the Constitution, the corresponding terms became "federalist" and "anti-federalist." As one author suggested, more than a little partisan strategy was involved in this fixing of political labels. Jackson Turner Main, *The Antifederalists—Critics of the Constitution, 1781-1788* (Chapel Hill: University of North Carolina Press, 1961), p. xi.

[2] The details of Pinckney's plan are obscure, though it appeared to have had much in common in provisions and philosophy with the Virginia Plan. In any event, his plan did not figure prominently in the debates. Cf. J. Franklin Jameson, "Studies in the History of the Federal Convention of 1787," *Annual Reports of the American Historical Association*, Vol. 1 (1902), (Washington, D.C.: Government Printing Office, 1903), p. 94.

[3] John P. Roche, "The Founding Fathers: A Reform Caucus in Action," *American Political Science Review*, Vol. 55 (1961), p. 805.

completed the outlines of a new government. On June 10 and 11 they settled upon a scheme of ratification, and went even the last step of agreeing that representation in the upper house as well as the lower house should be proportioned to population. The nationalist cause seemed victorious.

At this point the Convention adjourned "that leisure might be given for the purpose" of second thoughts on the subject of what had indeed been resolved and accomplished.[4] "Second thoughts" seems too mild a way of putting it, for by then many of the delegates were aghast at the arrangements to which they seemed committed. Luther Martin, Elbridge Gerry, William Paterson, and several other delegates from New York, New Jersey, Connecticut, and North Carolina declared the Convention unwise to go so far beyond the Articles, especially upon untried principles. More specifically, they said that no such scheme would be acceptable to the states. John Dickinson of Delaware said to Madison, "You see the consequence of pushing things too far."[5] In any event, a federalist opposition had appeared. When, accordingly, William Paterson asked leave to propose a "purely Federal" plan, moderate men of the nationalist persuasion—Washington and Franklin—strongly supported the motion.[6]

The "Federal" plan—the New Jersey Plan—that was reported began with the preamble: "That the Articles of Confederation ought to be . . . revised, corrected, and enlarged. . . ." In fact, the Plan altered the Articles very little, except to provide for amendments that had long been the subjects of discussion in the states or in Congress. It called for the establishment of a "supreme tribunal," but made no provision for inferior tribunals or for direct federal enforcement except by calling forth "the power of the Confederated states." It provided for taxation, but mostly for "external" taxes or duties, and left the arrangements for collection up to the Congress. Most particularly, it was a "purely Federal" plan: the central government rested on the states. Congress would be composed of an equal representation from the states and the federal executive was removable either by the Congress or by application of the state executives. This plan was, no doubt, closer to what the delegates had originally supposed was expected from them; but it was a far cry from the vision that had led many of them to Philadelphia and the hopes that had been aroused in the preceding fortnight.

For many days the Convention debated the merits of the two plans. The debate was largely fruitless, with much picking at detail, many lengthy speeches (which neither Madison nor anyone else bothered to

---

[4] Charles Warren, *The Making of the Constitution* (Boston: Little, Brown and Company, 1928), pp. 217-218; *Records,* Vol. I, pp. 240, 241.

[5] Warren, *op. cit.,* p. 218.

[6] *Ibid.,* p. 217.

SUMMARY OF PROVISIONS

THE VIRGINIA PLAN (RANDOLPH RESOLUTIONS)*

1. A National Legislature of two branches (houses) with representation proportioned either to the quotas of contribution or to the number of free inhabitants.

   The members of the second branch to be elected by the first from persons nominated by the State Legislatures; to receive such salary and hold term for such times as will insure their independence; and to be ineligible for any office established by a State of under the United States (except legislative office).

   Congress to have the power: to legislate where "the separate States are incompetent," or where "the harmony of the United States may be interrupted by the exercise of individual legislation,"; to negative any laws contravening the articles of union; and to have the power to call forth the "force of the Union" against any recalcitrant member.

2. A National Executive to be elected by the Legislature for a fixed term of years and to be ineligible for re-election.

3. A Council of Revision composed of the Executive and members of the Judiciary to review acts of the National Legislature and particular state legislatures and to exercise a suspensive veto over these acts.

4. A National Judiciary to include a "supreme tribunal" and inferior tribunals chosen by the Legislature, but to serve during good behavior; to have jurisdiction over admiralty, diversity of citizenship cases, cases involving collection of the national revenues, impeachment of national officers, and "questions which involve the national peace and harmony."

5. Provision to be made for the admission of new states; a guarantee of the territory of each state and of a republican government to each state.

6. The Legislative, Executive, and Judiciary officers in each state to be bound by oath to support the articles of Union.

---

* Since there are four texts reported for the Randolph Resolutions, no summary can be entirely authoritative. Most authors, however, seem to agree substantially upon the most important provisions. See Warren, *op. cit.*, p. 140*n;* also Jameson, *op. cit.*, p. 103.

SUMMARY OF PROVISIONS
THE NEW JERSEY PLAN (PATERSON RESOLUTIONS)

1. The Congress to consist of one house in which representation was to be by states.
   Congress to have the power, subject to the concurrence of a number (unstated) of states to: levy duties on foreign goods, impose stamp taxes and postal fees, and make rules and regulations for their collection; regulate foreign and interstate commerce; make requisitions in proportion to the number of white inhabitants and "three-fifths of other persons . . ." except Indians not paying taxes, and to devise provisions for collection from non-complying states.
2. A plural Executive to be elected by Congress for a term of years and to be removable either by Congress or by application of a majority of the Executives of the states.*
   The Executive to have the power to: appoint federal officers and direct military operations (provided that no member of the executive personally take command of any troops).
3. A supreme tribunal (no inferior federal tribunals) appointed by the executive and holding office during good behavior.
   The supreme tribunal to have jurisdiction over the impeachment of federal officers, cases involving the law of nations, treaties, regulation of trade, or collection of federal revenue (jurisdiction in the latter two categories only in the last instance).
4. All laws or treaties of the United States to be the law of the respective states and the judiciary of the states to be bound by them; the federal Executive authorized to "call forth the power of the Confederated States . . ." to compel obedience.
5. Provision to be made for the admission of new states, for a uniform rule of naturalization, and for a fair trial within each state of offenses committed by citizens of other states.

* The New Jersey Plan provided for a plural executive. The number of the executive was not made explicit in the Virginia Plan. Randolph favored a plural executive (Warren, *op. cit.*, p. 77); but one draft of the Resolutions also specified a single executive (Jameson, *op. cit.*, p. 109). When James Wilson moved that there be a single president the delegates recognized the step to be a decisive one. (Warren, *op. cit.*, pp. 173-74; Jameson, *op. cit.*, p. 109).

report), and a good bit of high-flown oratory. At the end of two weeks, no progress seemed to have been made and the Convention was at an impasse, with Washington and several others close to despair. Yet if the delegates accomplished nothing else, they at least discovered what was fundamental to each party. Just as the opening two weeks appeared to educate the federalists and the small-state representatives about what they could not tolerate, so the two weeks of debate over the New Jersey Plan may have made clear to both sides that a formula for compromise was needed; that if there were to be a Constitution, that constitution must incorporate more than one philosophy. Finally, with only Wilson and Madison irreconcilably opposed, the Convention agreed upon the appointment of a Compromise Committee.

Five days later the Committee reported, and after another ten days of debate, the essential provisions of the Connecticut Compromise were adopted: popular representation in the lower house; equal representation in the upper; and the origin of all money bills in the lower house. The Compromise satisfied no one entirely. The simple formula that it established was, furthermore, only a beginning: a decisive step, but no more than an outline of a solution. Nevertheless, the Convention made steady progress from that point. At no time after its adoption was there a serious danger that the delegates might break apart. Nor did they undo the Compromise; their deliberations moved with a greater sureness, the outlines of the governmental scheme were sharpened, and powers and limitations were clearly articulated.

Because the Connecticut Compromise was dramatic and critical—the product of a sharp confrontation of opposing constitutional theories and political commitments—it is often taken as representing the resolution of the federal question. This conclusion is far from the truth. The Connecticut Compromise was only the first of a series of arrangements essentially federal in character, several of less importance but a few nearly as significant as the "Grand Compromise" itself. Important among these other provisions were the "three-fifths clause" (by which three-fifths of the slaves were to be counted for representation and taxation) and the electoral college formula to elect the President. The provision for admitting new states entailed a sectional compromise, as did the power to regulate foreign and domestic commerce. Even the provision for a judicial review of state laws was in part a federal arrangement, since it was an alternative to legislative veto or executive force. These provisions filled in the bare sketch of a settlement indicated by the Connecticut Compromise. As the structure grew, as the delegates moved forward from the Compromise and built upon it, giving a specific character to the arrangements of the federal system and the national government, their satisfaction with the results increased.

With respect to the Connecticut Compromise, two facts are both striking and curious. First, the clash over the two plans was dramatic and fundamental, yet little has been said in discussions of the Convention about the nature of the division of the two parties and the reasons for such fundamental opposition. Second, the Compromise seemed an obvious one; yet the debate went on for two weeks, and the disagreement was so basic that the Convention almost gave up the task of drafting a constitution. The most plausible hypothesis is that the delegates were, at least in part, exploring the character and the dimensions of their own disagreements. In any event, we are left to reconstruct what, from a philosophical point of view, was at stake.

The dispute leading to the Connecticut Compromise has usually been treated as a large state–small state issue. To a considerable extent it was, for Virginia, Pennsylvania, and Massachusetts were ranged against Connecticut, Maryland, and Delaware. There was a frank and open fear on the part of the small-state delegates that a few large states led by Virginia—the Prussia of the Confederation—would control the union. The fear persisted despite Madison's sage observation that these several states, with their differing and separate interests in tobacco, flour, and fish, staple products and manufactures, had little desire over the long term for a combination at the expense of the other states.[7]

Divisions and alignments that cut across the differences between the large and the small states were also important. New York, despite its size and strategic position, sided with the small states. South Carolina and Georgia, not obviously in either camp, sided with the large states. Once the Compromise was adopted, Ellsworth and Dickinson as well as several other small-state delegates became unionists, while others such as Gerry and Mason rejected the Constitution (largely because of its federal arrangements) despite an earlier acceptance. The small state–large state division marked only one kind of dispute; if the Convention action upon federal arrangements is interpreted only according to the size of the states several deep-lying differences are lost.[8]

Two lines of cleavage marked fundamental differences of political theory dividing the delegates: one a matter of ideals; the other a matter of political prophesy or of beliefs about political behavior. The competing ideals—those of federalist and nationalist—were supported by different views of political behavior, especially of the importance of specific institutionalized checks upon government and of the value of direct political accountability versus the efficacy of social, cultural, and economic forces working toward unity and harmony.

In the nationalist camp were those men associated with the calling of the Federal Convention and the making of the Constitution itself:

---

[7] Warren, *op. cit.*, p. 250.

[8] See especially Andrew C. McLaughlin, *The Confederation and the Constitution* (New York and London: Harper and Brothers Publishers, 1905), pp. 217 ff.

Washington, Madison, Hamilton, Charles Pinckney, Benjamin Franklin, James Wilson, and Gouverneur Morris. They differed in many ways, but as a group they foresaw a nation welded together by common rights and common economic activity and interest. Freedom and equal rights in an expanding, agrarian republic was the Madisonian vision: a nation whose government could enforce equal rights throughout the land, and that would be a friend to the immigrant and generous parent-by-adoption to all the citizens of the western states.[9] In Madison's eyes, access to the land and equal rights were the cardinal tenets. At an opposite end was the economic nationalism of Hamilton or Gouverneur Morris, both of whom frankly avowed their preference for mercantile and commercial pursuits, the intellectually quickened and thriving character of such activities, and the "busy haunts of man" that they nourished.[10] Between these extremes would be found, for example, Washington, who despite his agrarian background continually urged commercial collaboration among the states in the interests of national unity.[11] The differences among the nationalists were real enough, and they were felt in such matters as commerce, external tariffs, slavery, and the admission of western states. Yet underlying their differences was a common thread: that a national citizenship—and indeed a nation—could be built upon men's common interest in equal laws, abundant opportunity, and thriving activity.

In the Convention, for the most part, the opposition to the nationalist point of view as an articulated philosophy took mostly the form of dire prophesies of a "consolidation," the tyranny of several states over the many, or declamations that the states would most certainly reject the Constitution.[12] The federalists appear to have been caught unprepared and without a ready response. Yet their fears and their opposition were definite and powerful; and if their opposition on theoretical grounds in the Convention was less than clear, the underlying philosophy became much more defined in the state ratifying conventions.

The federalist opposition to centralization did not rest upon the grounds that one is usually given to expect. For instance, the federalists were not stout believers in local democracy. Luther Martin, Elbridge Gerry, and others of their faction did not especially love democrats or democratic ways. They were not especially sensitive, either, to the pains of debtors nor the claims of paper money advocates. Nor were they

---

[9] See especially *Records,* Vol. II, pp. 123-24, 268-69. Consider also the inscription on the Statue of Liberty: ". . . Give me your tired, your poor, your huddled masses yearning to breathe free / The wretched refuse of your teeming shore . . ."

[10] The phrase is Gouverneur Morris's.

[11] Warren, *op. cit.,* pp. 34-35.

[12] *Records,* Vol. I, pp. 150-180; 196-200.

devotees of the grassroots or worshippers of a bucolic Arcadia.[13] For that matter, nationalists such as Hamilton and Morris were strongly attached to the notion of powerful local constituencies and governments, and Madison and Pinckney advocated physiocracy[14] and rural society. In Virginia's ratifying convention a federalist such as Patrick Henry would invoke the image of a toil-worn farmer enjoying his well-earned rest surrounded by wife and sturdy sons to articulate his state's opposition to the Constitution; in Massachusetts the federalist appeal was likely to be to the opposite—a thriving local commercialism, small in scale but achieving a higher level of energy and virtue than a more extensive government.[15] Indeed, much more than personalty versus realty, Arcadia versus urban commercial society, or even large state versus small state, the issue was local sovereignty and political attachments *versus* a new kind of politics depending upon untried political arrangements and incalculable social and economic forces. A root issue for the federalist was, simply: why ought control over our affairs be delegated? and how, once delegated, can the governmental power that is created be curbed and contained?

Along with the fear of a new "layer" of government manifested in the Convention, there appeared in the opponents of ratification within the state conventions another, competing ideal to the nationalist program for union: a philosophy of "purely federal" principles, enunciated by such men as Patrick Henry of Virginia, Melancthon Smith of New York, and several individuals in Massachusetts.[16] Their views are of interest not only because they are a coherent alternative to the proposed union on nationalist principles, but also because of the light they shed on present constitutional arrangements.

One part of the federalist sentiment was simply fear of an external power that might be unresponsive to and unconscious of local needs. Throughout the Convention the delegates expressed doubts that "so diverse" a people could be governed under a common head. They feared

---

[13] Arcadia was a district in ancient Greece cited as the ideal of rural contentment. For a good documentation of the federalist opposition, see Cecilia M. Kenyon, "Men of Little Faith: The Anti-Federalists on the Nature of Representative Government," *William and Mary Quarterly,* Vol. 12 (1955), pp. 3-43. See also, for an opposing view, Main, *op. cit.*

[14] A doctrine that land is the source of all wealth and agrarian values ought to guide government policy.

[15] Jonathan Elliott, *Debates in the Several State Conventions on the Adoption of the Federal Constitution* (Philadelphia: J. B. Lippincott Co., 1901), 2d ed., Vol. II, pp. 136ff., and Vol. III, p. 54. Hereafter cited as Elliott.

[16] The "federal" philosophy did not suddenly spring into being in the controversy over adoption. Its antecedents go back at least to 1781 and the issue of the Impost, at which time partisans put forward principles and theories of government similar to the nationalist and federalist ones that figures in the Convention and the ratification. See Main, *op. cit.*, pp. xi, 121.

a combination of the large states that would monopolize the advantages of union. Southerners feared the north and the east feared a rising west. Much of the delegates' interest was in a common power to regulate commerce, to tax, and to support general navigation laws; yet they feared these powers. Underlying all was the realistic view that political collectivities take what they can get: that a state will, for the benefit of its citizens and the happy and comfortable life of its officials, monopolize the trade of a neighbor, sell off another's lands, tax according to a principle of self-preference, and look out first and last for its own.

Coupled with this fear of an external force and hostile political combinations was a distaste, especially in the state conventions, for entrusting the community's interests to the "virtual" representation[17] of a cosmopolitan national elite not responsive to the local area's sentiments, social condition, and economic interest. They feared (or said they feared) the "lawyers and men of learning, and moneyed men, that talk so finely and gloss over matters so smoothly, to make us poor illiterate people swallow down the pill."[18] In a large empire, argued the federalist opposition in the state conventions, the lesser people cannot concert; they are at a disadvantage, subject to those who can act "over their heads" on a national level. Their representatives must therefore be close to them. They should, said Melancthon Smith of New York, "be a true picture of the people, possess a knowledge of their circumstances and their wants, sympathize in all their distresses, and be disposed to seek their true interests.[19] To insure that they do all these things, said Mason in the Virginia Convention, the representative ought frequently to return to the people, live among them, and "participate their burdens."[20]

The dislike of the federalist for a cosmopolitan elite seems to have been supported by a genuine fear of tyranny: of tax collectors and their agents acting locally but without local sanction; of harsh decrees from a federal court; of a standing army that would displace the local militia. More practical and immediate fears were that the poor would pay the taxes; that power would gravitate from hands of the people; that redress through the courts would be removed to a distant seat.

A good case can be made that the federalist opposition was founded upon self-interest, antipathy to change, and a crabbed distrust of political

---

[17] Virtual Representation: "representation founded upon a vaguely drawn subjective constituency with little active power." Alfred de Grazia, *Public and Republic* (New York: Alfred A. Knopf, 1951), p. 14. Virtual representation is contrasted both to elective representation and to representation in which *all delegated powers* of government exercised by the representative (as agent) are specifically and peremptorily controlled by the electorate (as principal) in a definite and democratically constituted territorial constituency.

[18] Mr. Amos Singleterry of Massachusetts (who was far from ignorant or illiterate). Elliott, Vol. II, p. 101.

[19] *Ibid.*, p. 245.

[20] *Ibid.*, Vol. III, p. 496.

power.[21] Many state and anti-Convention revolutionary leaders were old in contrast to the notable youthfulness of the leading Convention factions.[22] In the states, many anti-unionists did speak for a well-entrenched set of local influentials who were satisfied with things as they were and ill-disposed to see political arrangements scrambled.[23] Above all else, the opposition to a strong union, both in Philadelphia and in the state conventions, distrusted centralized political or administrative power, certainly when it was not controlled nor controllable by local groups in an immediate and peremptory fashion. Paradoxically, despite their appeals to the local constituency and to the exercise of popular home rule, the federalist cause seems a conservative one, distrustful of change and of human nature.

Power is seldom claimed, however, without an ideal for which it stands, falsely or faithfully. There appears to have been such a definite ideal behind many of the federalist objections, touched upon in Convention and made much clearer in the states, especially by Patrick Henry, Melancthon Smith, Luther Martin, and Elbridge Gerry. Today, their ideal seems distant and strange, because we are greatly removed from it. But it was not strange to the federalist opposition, nor to their countrymen, nor to their century. It had much in common with the federal republics prescribed by Montesquieu and Rousseau: and though the Articles had few articulate theorists to support it, the ideal of the federalist opposition seems very much to represent the principles and political goods that might have been sought under a reformed Articles. That ideal can be described as a limited contractual union of republics, each practicing locally its own version of civic virtue.

A local regime of virtue was pictured by some as Arcadia and by others on a more urban model of honest mechanics and artisans, thriving business, pious learning, and sound principles of household management. But the ideal was in no sense romantic democracy, either urban or rustic. Nor did it seem to entail great sympathy for debtors and the dispossessed except in states such as North Carolina, where the whole area was impoverished and money poor. Certainly what was being asserted was the right of each community to take care of its "own," but the notion of a local regime of virtue conveyed other important ideas: a tie between benefit and responsibility; and effective social controls, stimuli and checks to elicit both civic energy and responsiveness to common concerns. "Local virtue" meant simply and plausibly, given the prevailing social and economic conditions, that people would behave more like citizens, that

[21] Cf. Cecilia M. Kenyon, *op. cit.*

[22] Stanley Elkins, and Eric McKitrick, "The Founding Fathers—Young Men of the Revolution," *Political Science Quarterly*, Vol. 76 (1961), pp. 181-218. Main denies that age differentials were important. *Op. cit.*, p. 259.

[23] Cf. Forrest McDonald, *We The People—The Economic Origins of the Constitution* (Chicago: Chicago University Press, 1958), especially Ch. 2.

there would in fact be more justice, when communities acted on their own behalf rather than delegating their problems to a higher constituency.

The argument was, in a sense, that charity begins at home, but it had a sound foundation. People did not see society as naturally harmonious, particularly without such "built-in" social and political regulators as the automatic market mechanism, bonds between localities, and ties between leaders and localities. It was natural to assume that any "virtue" that could be realized had to be realized locally. Locally, the community could assert itself. Locally, the government's accountability to the populace could be enforced. Following this philosophy, the federal system that would make sense was one of contractually associated communities, not some such creation as James Wilson's "popular pyramid."

Patrick Henry and several others in the state conventions even took the offensive by proposing as an alternative to the suggested Constitution a republic modeled upon true federal principles: an American version of the Swiss Confederation or the United Dutch Provinces. Here, they said, were splendid enough models: local liberties, virtuous citizens, a republican self-defense coupled with a love of peace. The life of these republics was precarious, but so was liberty. They were not powerful as nations, but there was vigor in the associated members. They were small republics; but better republicanism on a small scale than continental expansion that might bring consolidation or monarchy. By indirection they asked of the pro-Constitution nationalists, "What, fellow citizens, are your true aims: are they liberty and republicanism; or are they, perhaps, expansion and glory?"

In the Convention itself, the federalist opposition made a poor case. They were few in number, many of their strongest adherents having remained at home. Their own examples were turned against them, Madison and Wilson pointing out that along with republican virtue Switzerland and Holland also provided examples of local oligarchy, communal rioting, trade wars, and ultimate dictatorship. More to the immediate problems, their projected ideals of a refurbished Articles could not insure "commutative justice between the states," a common and growing commerce, or power against external threats. Whether the federalists' ideal ought to have died or not, it was on the merits of the debate put down.

These two philosophies—nationalist and federalist—make clear the critical role of the Connecticut Compromise. Fundamental and passionately held theories of government were at stake. They involved ultimate values: the expanded vision of a great nation participating in common rights and prosperity versus the principles of independence, civic virtue, and the precarious venture of liberty. Compromise was the only solution. The justice on both sides and the absence of a higher unity that would reconcile both philosophies argued, as Franklin observed, that the delegates must "make a joint."[24]

The Connecticut Compromise also fit the conditions of eighteenth-century politics. Only a compromise could give security against the disastrous extremes of consolidation or dissolution. The nationalists demanded popular representation, the federalists representation by states. In support of the nationalist cause, Madison argued two theses: diversity of primary producer interests made political combination unlikely; and common sentiments of justice and patriotism were more important than a specific distribution of political power. American history, especially in the early years, showed how dubious was the first proposition. And a moment's reflection would expose the fallacy of the second. The American community lacked intergroup and intersectional ties. It lacked the controls and incentives, and the "alternate resources,"[25] afforded by a modern economy. It lacked connecting links of influence between the central government and the localities and between national and local leaders. It lacked, therefore, the bases for a moderate and temperate majority will. Consequently, a substitute had to be found, and in this respect the federalists were upon unassailable ground. Given the political circumstances, an alternate method of representation was in itself advisable. And, directly to the point, the distribution of *formal* political power was essential to assure constitutional, responsive, and accountable government. It was so important precisely because other modes of influence were relatively ineffective.

The preceding argument establishes the federalist case, but also cuts against it. True, a defense for the states against the Union (and the interests and civic virtue they represented and protected) required a separate representation. But the Union also required a political support of its own. The argument was that American politics tended toward faction: people and groups got through politics what could not be gained by other means; and when their other means were scanty the temptation to seek a political solution was strong. If a group could not by persuasion, organizational power, or economic resource realize its goals, the political weapon was the alternative. Thus, protect the states from the nation. From this argument, however, it also follows that the nationalist case is equally solid: a representation by states alone, coupled with local autonomy, would speedily erupt into destructive political competition and possibly armed conflict and disunion.

---

[24] *Records,* Vol. I, p. 488.

[25] Cf. Alexis de Tocqueville, *Democracy in America,* Vol. II, Bk. 2. The concept of "alternate resources" is put forward and discussed in relation to contemporary American democracy especially by Robert A. Dahl. See *Who Governs?* (New Haven: Yale University Press, 1961), especially Bk. IV.

We have said that the Compromise did little more than settle the outlines of a federal solution. The specific character of American federalism was set by a series of agreements and bargains concluded over a month later in the Convention, only after basic differences over the Congress and the Presidency had been resolved. In establishing the outlines of a federal solution, however, the Connecticut Compromise was of great importance. It associated two political principles: sectional diversity and national vigor. Most immediately this association was expressed in the formula for a popularly elected House and a Senate with equal representation for the states. The same principles also appeared later in the Presidency: a single executive, elected by a college of state representatives, but powerful and independent and eligible to succeed himself. Both the treaty and the appointive powers included the same elements of unified power and responsiveness to sectional interests. In lesser measure, arrangements dealing with commerce, the judiciary, and the military establishment were also determined by the logic of the Grand Compromise. Thus the federal system itself became a part of, a supplement to, and supplemented by, the representative arrangements of the Constitution. The federal system also became a part of the system of checks and balances by which the central government and its separate branches were to be restrained.

The Compromise also determined that the Constitution would include *both* the nationalist and the federalist philosophies of citizenship and of politics. This bargain was not explicitly made, but the delegates, in other federal arrangements, honored the implicit understanding. Thus, the Constitution incorporated provisions that fostered the national citizenship so close to the hopes of Madison, Wilson, Hamilton, and Washington. But the Constitution also gave ample scope for local political autonomy, for a politics rooted in the communities, close to the average citizen and to his political understanding and personal experience.

As yet the principles of sectional diversity and national vigor had not been fitted into a working political scheme of central government. And the dual citizenship established by the Compromise was not as yet connected and reconciled.

The Bonds of Union

Immediately following the Connecticut Compromise, the Convention debated representation, the federal judiciary, the Congress, and the Presidency. These subjects occupied the delegates for the next three weeks. On August 6, a Committee of Detail reported on the powers of Congress, including most of the provisions of the Articles, but adding a series of prohibitions limiting the states and providing Congress with wide power over the military establishment, taxation, and commerce.[26] These issues were to occupy the Convention for much of its remaining time and to require additional bargains, especially between the east and north and the south.[27]

Three broad issues of federalism were opened with the Report of August 6. For Madison and Pinckney, Morris and Wilson, and several federalists as well, fundamental questions of national citizenship and of the primary bonds of intersectional unity now arose concretely, in the arrangements to be made about new states, commerce, taxation, and representation. In dealing with these issues and with the powers of central government, the delegates had to discover strategies for social and economic progress that would not overload the central political system with more group and sectional conflict than it could support. They had to find ways to decentralize conflict or delegate it to neutral (nonpolitical) agencies. Finally, and especially as a directly practical matter of securing acceptance of the Constitution, the delegates had to strike sectional bargains, to distribute the sectional "spoils."

Even when the delegates were debating the Connecticut Compromise, one pattern of sectional conflict had already emerged that went to the fundamental question of the primary bonds of citizenship for the new nation. On July 14, the very day that the Congress of the Articles adopted the Northwest Ordinance, the Convention found itself sharply divided over the admission of new states. All the delegates were vitally concerned with providing for a future nation, for their descendants and the millions that would ultimately inhabit the vast territories of the west. They disagreed over which provisions to make. For one section, the south, the citizen would be an American primarily through participating in equal rights under the law, breathing the air of a free republican government, and enjoying the opportunity to take up land and be independent. Madison argued that the West would serve as an escape from European tyranny and from the social density and inequality that would be bred in the east. But in the eastern and central states, this vision of republicanism, physiocratic principles, and an expanding agrarian empire was disquieting. Aside from the important fact that they were land poor, had few western lands, and feared a political combination between the south and the west to their detriment, some easterners also saw the commerce and the urban, cosmopolitan values of the east threatened by a leveling and populistic spirit in the future west.[28]

---

[26] *Records,* Vol. II, pp. 176-187.

[27] For the debates in Convention, see *Records,* especially Vol. II, pp. 355-78, 408-21, 435-44.

[28] Especially Gouverneur Morris and Elbridge Gerry. See *Records,* Vol. I. p. 604; Vol. II, pp. 2, 3.

Hard upon the issue of Western lands came that of commerce. The east wanted Congress to regulate trade and to provide for the navigation laws so essential to their prosperity. For many of the eastern delegates this power was almost the *raison d'etre* for the Convention itself. Knowing commerce to be vulnerable to political attacks upon property or economic expectations, they feared the voting power of agrarians, especially if those "agrarians" included (for enumeration) slaves as well as yeoman. On the other hand the south, and also several states of the east and north, opposed any arrangement that allowed a favored few to act the part Britain had earlier. They objected even more to giving Congress the power to allow a trade monopoly either across the seas or inland from the east. Just as southerners felt themselves defenseless where the "terms of trade" could be so readily turned against them, so they also felt their agrarian economy especially vulnerable to direct taxation and tariffs.

The issues of taxation, commerce, and representation (enumeration) brought to a head the question of slavery and especially of slavery in the future.[29] Earlier, little had been said upon the subject. A few northerners had declared slavery and the slave trade an abomination. Pinckney had responded that so long as rice and indigo land in South Carolina needed to be cleared, he would not hear of a prohibition of the trade. The question of slavery had not, however, received a general hearing. With the concrete problems of numbers and representation, taxation, and external trade to resolve, the future of slavery and especially of the slave trade could no longer be kept quietly in the background. The delegates were forced to put principle against principle, union against freedom and unsullied republicanism, and to declare their stand.

They proceeded cautiously and empirically, seeming to work almost by a tacit method of group and sectional bargaining. The sectional compromises were tested, in turn, against the evolving pattern of central government. At one point, the Convention resorted again to a compromise committee to deal especially with the issues of representation, taxation, and commerce. Ultimately, the delegates arrived at another "grand" group of compromises, closely related to each other and especially vital to the character of American federalism. These compromises can be summarized as follows:

1. A unified national power to regulate commerce, with the proviso that there be no state taxation of imports or federal taxation of exports.

---

[29] The disposition of Western lands might have also raised the issue, but it did not. Under the Northwest Ordinance, states were to be admitted on a footing of equality. That provision implied that the choice of free or slave was a matter for the state. The Convention gave to Congress power to fix conditions for entry, contrary to the Northwest Ordinance, but not because of a desire to limit slavery.

2. Direct taxation to be apportioned according to population and all excises to be uniform.
3. Slave population to be counted at three-fifths both for taxation and representation.[30]
4. Congress empowered to impose conditions on the admission of new states.
5. The slave trade to continue until 1808 (for 20 years).

What is obvious about the great intersectional bargain over slavery, commerce, and taxation—aside from the fact that no one interest got its full schedule of demands—is that it incorporated fundamental compromises of principle that affected the future character of the nation. For the delegates, commerce and taxation, equal laws and the protection of property were matters of economic interest; they were also the binding arrangements that tied the citizenry together, and determined the character of American federalism.

The commerce clause was the most notable of the compromises. Initially the issue for the delegates was not that of a general commerce clause, but the power of Congress to provide for navigation acts. At the prospect of navigation laws, the South became alarmed and demanded a two-thirds vote in Congress as a protection, Pinckney adding that such a vote should be a condition for *any* act touching commerce. With a prohibition of federal taxation on exports this demand was abandoned.[31] At the same time, state taxation of imports was prohibited entirely. This was a brave act representing a triumph for the nationalist faction, for a good many states had reasons to fear imports from their neighbors—wheat and flour from New Jersey, the manufactures of Pennsylvania, the timbers of Georgia and Maine. The Congressional power of regulating commerce as a whole, coupled with a prohibition upon impairing the obligation of contract and issuing paper money, carried farther the notion of a people united in a common national prosperity.

Despite other features of the compromise, the Madisonian vision of equal opportunity in the expanding agrarian republic survived in large measure. Congress was free to impose conditions upon new states entering the Union, violating the principle that Madison and other southerners

---

[30] The "three-fifths" formula was not new. It had been recommended by Congress in their resolution of April 18, 1783 and had become known as the "Federal Ratio." The Convention, however, tied both representation and direct taxation to the formula.

[31] This item has commonly escaped notice: the prohibition of a federal export tax. The delegates were attempting, immediately, to prevent the preferential treatment of the ports or external commerce of a given state (as well as a tax upon the export of slaves). In addition, perhaps unwittingly, they were abandoning the principles of national mercantilism, taking, long before the mother country and, indeed, first among nations, a decisive step toward free international trade, and removing the issue of a national policy of provision and monopoly from federal politics.

sought.[32] The Constitution did adopt the principle implicit in the Ordinances of 1786 and 1787: that the western territories and future territories of the Union should be treated as a public and national domain, open for the settlement of succeeding generations. States were also enjoined to grant to the citizens of each state the "privileges and immunities of the citizens of the several states," and to accord to a sister state "full faith and credit to all their public acts, deeds, and records." The Constitution established republican government and civil equality, along with the promise of abundance, as the inheritance of the citizen. For the settler and the citizen it offered equal opportunity, even a second chance for the unlucky, the disadvantaged, or their successors.

By setting the formulae for taxation and enumeration the delegates were providing assurances of protection to the states and especially to agrarians. They were limiting the politics of intersectional bargaining and coalition. The three-fifths clause secured a reasonably equal distribution of primary political power among states and sections. The restrictions upon taxation limited the scope of potential struggle over the distribution of sectional costs and benefits.[33] By further withdrawing commerce from state and sectional contention they carried this philosophy another step and provided also for a steady and powerful influence to erase sources of conflict. Their strategy was both to limit and to make possible a politics of sectionalism.

The delegates provided for union, for a moderate politics of sectionalism, for strength in the central government and vitality in its parts. They also nourished a generous vision of American citizenship. That vision did not include the Negro slave. Indeed, according to a later generation of abolitionists, the delegates bought union and liberty for the white man at the price of slavery for the black. And though they did not deliberately make a "covenant with death and an agreement with hell," the case for the Convention is a bad one. The delegates, with virtually no debate, accepted a fugitive slave law. They provided for a continuance of the slave trade for twenty years. And they left open the issue of whether new states would be slave or free. Many seemed to suppose that slavery was dying in the face of economic and humanitarian sentiment. Perhaps a few truly wanted a slave empire. However these matters may be, the fact remains that the Constitution paved the way to an entrenchment of the "peculiar institution," to Bloody Kansas, and to Dred Scott.

---

[32] The power granted to Congress was, Madison said, a "compensation" to Pennsylvania and especially to Gouverneur Morris. Apparently it was granted not from a distaste for slavery but as a protection to eastern commerce. See Warren, *op. cit.*, p. 596; *Records,* Vol. II, p. 458.

[33] For this point I am especially indebted to Professor Charles E. Gilbert of the Department of Political Science, Swarthmore College. See also, James M. Buchanan and Gordon Tullock, *The Calculus of Consent—Logical Foundations of Constitutional Democracy* (Ann Arbor: The University of Michigan Press, 1962), Ch. 10.

Federalism and Democracy

Patently, the problems that perplexed the Founding Fathers trouble us still. Still we struggle to reconcile within one frame of government sectionalism, local autonomy, and common rights. So, too, we work with a federalism which, though greatly changed, is still the recognizable descendent of the system as they conceived it.

For the Convention delegates, the key premise of the federal solution was the proposition that the potential for group and sectional conflict in the United States was high. They believed also that a diverse country could not by direct political attack upon political issues resolve the fundamental differences of interest and sentiment that separated the American people into many sections and factions. For them, consequently, moderating sectional collisions and strengthening the bonds of unity were overridingly important.

A successful federalism for them entailed a substantial separation of local and national democracy. As James Wilson argued, the union that they made was not a "popular pyramid," not a whole possessed of a common moral will. The delegates provided for a firm central government and desired also vigorous local government; but for both immediate political reasons and because of philosophical conviction they accepted only a small part of the Wilsonian philosophy of a popular pyramid. They attempted to provide instead for a moderate intersectional politics. And, especially with respect to federal arrangements, they sought to "sublimate" sectional conflict by relying upon a strategy of national economic unification[34] and a growing common citizenship.

The delegates erred in some of their calculations; and in this respect the comment of critics like Beard and Smith is pertinent. We have already noted the delegates' disastrous miscalculation—if it may be called that—on the slave question. And it would seem fair to say that these realistic and hardheaded statesmen expected too easy a synthesis of such ideals as property, abundance, and equal rights, wagered too readily that the future would erode fundamental conflicts.

In the minds of the delegates, the provision for a dual citizenship strengthened republican sentiments. The federal system permitted diversity of political and economic arrangements. With the representative provisions (see Chapter V) of the Constitution, it encouraged national responsiveness to local sentiments. It allowed the practice of local civic virtue—valuable practice for a country in which the political habits needed for self-government were not yet strongly established. At the same time, the more "cosmopolitan" citizenship favored by the nationalists could stand independently and also counter excessive parochialism.

---

[34] See especially Hamilton's comments in *The Federalist,* Numbers Twelve and Thirteen.

The delegates sought to capitalize upon the civic energies of Americans. The distribution and delegation of power within the federal system was, in part, a political necessity. It was also, even to nationalists like Gouverneur Morris and Alexander Hamilton, a virtue as well: contributing to a high level of political energy throughout the whole of the union. Similarly, the delegates understood that the American nation included sections and groups of great diversity. They sought to allow this diversity constructive political expression, recognizing that in giving play to contradiction and pragmatic adjustment they were expressing in part the "genius" of the American people.

The delegates also planned for a secure civic equality that had both an economic-social aspect and a legal or constitutional one: common prosperity and widely distributed opportunity; and a common enjoyment of rights and political status under an equal law. That plan was intended to supplement and "democratize" the politics of sectionalism. American citizens had equal primary political power, economic opportunity, and social mobility. The Founding Fathers were not social levelers. They defended property and the economy. But they also designed the Constitution to cooperate with and direct two of the most powerful motives of the modern era: the desire for free movement and the desire for individual betterment. They did so to strengthen the union and to provide for a common national citizenship. They did so, as well, to quicken the forces of economic development and social change.

The eighteenth-century philosopher Montesquieu wrote of a "spirit of the laws." The delegates themselves spoke of capturing the "genius of the American people." Expressions of this sort signified the need that statesmen felt to support the laws by establishing a close harmony between formal juridical provisions and influences latent in the polity. Americans have argued the question of whether the Founding Fathers did or did not effectively achieve that end. That argument, a continuing one, ought not to obscure the objective itself. It was the delegates' aim to use such forces as civic energy, social mobility, and economic enterprise for constitutional ends.

The delegates' constitutional method of withdrawal and delegation limited democracy as most understand it: for both federal and republican government had to be made secure. They also sought to provide for a united people and for great strength in the whole. While limiting the direct exercise of united political will the Founding Fathers provided for the future nation alternate resources to contribute to common solutions. These resources have often—as the Convention delegates anticipated—encouraged fresh vision and stimulated new political energies. They have also, at times, tempered political differences to the point where common solution is possible.

The American republic chose as a motto "E pluribus unum": from many, one. The Convention debates suggest how that motto was intended. From many small republics joined in a federation a nation ought to be created. The Founding Fathers provided a guide: not a prophesy of what would occur, but a design of government that could, with the efforts of statesmen, patriot leaders, and responsible citizens, reconcile progress, nationhood, and a republic within one constitutional system.

Chapter V

ORGANIZATION OF THE PUBLIC WILL

In considering the Randolph Resolutions the delegates touched upon almost all issues and institutions of government. But the Convention debates over the organization of the public will—suffrage and representation, the "powers" of government and their separation—acquired a quality of immediacy only with the resolution of the federal question by the Connecticut Compromise. The Compromise provided a steady guide point for the delegates, as did their fundamental agreement on republican government. But within these wide boundaries was ample scope for difference. Republican government meant government derived from and accountable to the populace. But derived how? and accountable in what manner? Most agreed that the government should have a more popular base and more political energy than the Congress of the Articles. But they faced the problem of how, specifically, to give it that base and that political energy. The government, republican as it would be, still needed an organized public will: a matter of specific arrangements with respect to representation, the powers of the branches of government, and the particular version of separation of powers to be adopted.

In proceeding, the delegates moved steadily but cautiously, balancing one constitutional provision against others. First, they agreed to a single executive elected for seven years by Congress. At the next stage, they regulated elections and the qualifications of voters and representatives. Then, in their attempt to settle the powers of Congress and the President, the issue of federalism erupted once again, producing the compromises over slavery and commerce. With those issues settled, the delegates were disposed to accept a President elected without a restriction upon succession and by an electoral college rather than the Congress. As a further concession to the federal principle, they provided for the participation of the Senate with the executive in both treaty-making and in appointments. Finally, on almost the last day of the Convention, the delegates agreed to a more popular base for representation in the House.[1]

In viewing the progress of the Convention, two tendencies stand out. One is the careful adjustment of republican government and federalism: the balancing of national political power with power in the units of the federal system. Another is the step-by-step countering of popular or public will with devices calculated to divide and check it.

Note, however, that with constitutional safeguards against the abuse of governmental power the delegates were willing to accord more to the populace, just as with a concession to popular authority they sought a check to or a distribution of political power.

Underlying the cautious arrangements in the constitutional scheme was a clash of fundamental philosophies. These philosophies were distinguished by sharp differences over the role of politics, the rationale of representation, and, finally, over the particular mainspring that ought to supply the dynamism of government itself.

Republicans and Monarchists

The preceding chapter discussed the important division between federalist and nationalist. Here, we deal with the organization of the public will, and another philosophic division comes to the fore: that between republican and "monarchist." The exemplar of republicanism was James Madison. Close to him were Washington, Randolph, Dickinson, and at times various of the "states' rights" delegates such as Gerry and Martin. The term "monarchist" is a hyperbole.[2] No one except perhaps Hamilton was truly a "monarchist." They were all republicans, although they maintained very different conceptions of republicanism. "Monarch-

---

[1] Responding to the only speech of direct political importance made by Washington.

[2] "Monarchist" was, however, widely used as an epithet, especially to designate the espousal of semidictatorial or antirepublican principles. During the Convention, one delegate (Mercer) kept a "score card," checking off those delegates he took to be "monarchist." See Charles Warren, *The Making of the Constitution* (Boston: Little, Brown and Company, 1928), p. 442.

ist" in this context designates a faction interested in centralist and *politically* vigorous government, from the tory democracy of Hamilton and Gouverneur Morris and the "executivism" of Robert Morris to the ideal of a "popular pyramid"[3] held by James Wilson and Benjamin Franklin.

To understand the pertinence of these two philoshopies, the concept of the "disharmonious society" is once again useful. Whether horizontal (or class) cleavages were important to the delegates is a matter of doubt. Colonial society enjoyed a large measure of equality. In Convention, Pinckney spoke of a "uniquely American" classlessness, and that view seems to have been shared.[4] On the other hand, the antipathies of creditor and debtor, of old family and new arrival, of gentlemen and yeomen were perceived by the delegates as important and as divisive. The delegates were conscious, then, of many *vertical* lines of cleavage. A famous statement of this same theme occurs in Number Ten of *The Federalist*, where Madison cites a "landed interest, a manufacturing interest, a mercantile interest, with many lesser interests . . ." as among the many sources of faction.[5]

A second problem for the delegates was the absence of effective communication from the small cluster of national politicians down to the local communities. A "grass-roots" antagonism toward the cosmopolitan national politicians accounted for part of the deficiency. Another reason was the absence of technical means and effective organization to communicate political views. Hamilton made this point in Number 84 of *The Federalist:*

> What are the sources of information . . . ? Of personal observation [the citizens] can have no benefit. This is confined to the citizens on the spot. They must therefore depend on the information of intelligent men in whom they confide; and how must these men obtain their information . . . from the complexion of public measures, from the public prints, from correspondence with representatives, and with other persons who reside at the place of their deliberations.

Thus, in America of the 1780's, political opinion about national affairs depended heavily upon personalities and individual communications. Correspondingly, the danger of a "political opinion" created by local demagogues and an irresponsible local press was high. Elbridge Gerry complained in the opening days of the Convention that the people "are the dupes of pretended patriots." "They are," he said, "daily misled into the most baneful measures and opinions by the false reports circulated by designing men, and which *no one on the spot can refute.*"[6] Here,

---

[3] Completed by a popularly elected and powerful President and Senate.

[4] Warren, *op. cit.*, p. 239-240; *Records*, Vol. I, pp. 400-01; also Louis Hartz, *The Liberal Tradition in America* (New York: Harcourt, Brace and Company, 1955).

[5] See also Robert E. Brown, *Charles Beard and the American Constitution* (Princeton: Princeton University Press, 1956), p. 30.

[6] *Records*, Vol. I, p. 48. Emphasis added.

then, was another aspect of the problem. Not only were means and organization lacking to make a national political will effective, but steps to counter this deficiency were urgent.

When the delegates faced the task of constructing the "representative republic," their principal theoretical disagreements were over how to deal with the "disharmonious polity." They disagreed in large measure on issues over which other republican theorists have differed.[7] The most important was how to treat the parts—constituencies, representatives, Congress and President—in order to make a whole and what kind of whole to make. For the republicans, the strategy was that of negating politics[8] by refining it with the impartial wisdom of patriots, sublimating it through neutral constitutional checks, and defeating it in the first instance by a wide representation of dissociated groups and interests. For the monarchist, the mere residuum that would survive the refining process was not enough: through politics a genuine corporate will must be created or the "whole" would break apart. The two parties were arguing an issue that Americans have perennially debated: how much politics is good for the country? Their debates included another, more practical issue: how best in the arrangements for representation, for public and legislative debate, and in the relations of executive and Congress, to provide for the emergence of a public will.

The monarchist faction was identified with the notion of a "corporate whole." Among the members of their group, however, two fairly distinct tendencies were represented. For one group, a "popular pyramid" seemed the most attractive. James Wilson was the most persistent and cogent exponent of this approach. He was seconded in his views, with greater and lesser consistency, by such men as Pinckney, Franklin, Mason, the two Morrises, and Hamilton. The purpose of the "popular pyramid," especially as expounded by Wilson, was to make the force of the national government felt directly throughout the land by an emphasis upon popular authority.[9]

On the juridical side, Wilson envisioned a broad array of Congressional and executive powers, a national court system, and a clear recognition of dual sovereignty, which to his mind meant primarily the power of direct action by the federal government upon the citizen. To support such a system Wilson argued for a numerous House of Representatives close in political style and feeling to those they represented, a single directly and popularly elected President, a Senate that represented numbers, and a broad, egalitarian suffrage.

---

[7] For example, Rousseau and Kant.

[8] "Politics" in the sense of influence and group bargaining, rather than statesmanship.

[9] For a good, brief summary of Wilson's views, see Charles Page Smith, *James Wilson—Founding Father* (Chapel Hill: Univ. of North Carolina Press, 1956), Chs. 15-17.

Wilson's bold leap toward a national democracy was far more than most of the delegates were prepared to support.[10] His scheme evaded the issue of a balance between the individual states and the states and the national government as a whole. Few aside from Wilson himself seemed to understand how such a system could work, especially with only a democratic political will as influence and support. In filling this deficiency of political support and will, another version of monarchist thought became especially important: the "national mercantilism" of Hamilton and a group of Eastern delegates such as the two Morrises, Mercer, Pierce, and King.[11]

Narrowly conceived, the Hamiltonian strategy was one of getting support for the government by activities designed to create mutual economic interests among groups and sections. Hamilton frankly said that the first aim of government should be to turn interest to its side.[12] With interest he included sentiment. Therefore, he would go a part of the way toward even democratic conceptions, supporting popular notions of liberty and arguing that free government would particularly enlist the passions of the community and beget public spirit and confidence in the political system.[13] More directly in line with his objective of "enlisting the passions," Hamilton put forward an ideal of the government as benevolent patron of commerce, manufactures, and mercantile prosperity. At a later point, in *The Federalist,* he also expounded a thesis similar to, though not precisely identical with Adam Smith's "harmony of interests."[14] In the Convention, he suggested that it was the business of government to make interest, individual and collective, the material of government both by becoming a "manager of prosperity" and by employing the power and patronage of the executive.

---

[10] The notion of a "popular pyramid" or a "democratic pyramid" may well have sounded Caesarist. One other statesman who made much of the concept was Louis Bonaparte. See Louis-Napoleon Bonaparte, *Des Idées Napoleoniennes* (Bruxelles: A. Wahlen et Cie., 1839).

[11] In the Convention itself, Hamilton actually played a limited role although his activities in encouraging the move toward the Convention and the adoption of the Constitution was a large one. Gouverneur Morris was probably the most influential "Hamiltonian" in the Convention itself.

[12] *Records,* Vol. I, p. 284.

[13] *Ibid.,* p. 145.

[14] Hamilton's argument was not the same as Adam Smith's. He did not, for example, speak of a providential hidden land, or the benevolent workings of free markets. He did argue for a potential compatibility of interests and for *ententes* of mutual profit. Thus, in Number Twelve of *The Federalist,* he proposed that government "multiply the means of gratification" by promoting the introduction of precious metals ("those darling objects of human avarice and enterprise"). He noted that taxes would rest more lightly upon all if money circulated freely. He suggested an additional mutual interest between commerce and industry: ". . . in proportion as commerce has flourished, land has risen in value." To his mind there was an opportunity and an impelling ground for government to "enlist the passions," and especially to do so by turning interest to its side.

Some of the Eastern mercantile set did not wholly share this Hamiltonian philosophy of positive government and national paternalism. Others, however, had preferences strongly inclining them to Hamilton's ideas. They saw that industry and commerce would be important in the future and wanted to foster their development. Some, like Gouverneur Morris, also disliked the Arcadian image and expressed a frank preference for industry, commerce, and the "busy haunts of man." A number also assumed that great differences of station and wealth ought to be accepted as an important consideration in designing the Constitution. Some argued that these differences were inevitable, some that they were desirable. They also, as a group, tended to deprecate disinterested patriotism as a political motive and to follow Hamilton in his counsels of "enlisting the passions." For all of these reasons, most of them were inclined to believe that promotional activities of government and a preference for trade and industry, though they might foster corruption, would on balance produce more good than evil, stimulate activity, foster a hearty and cheery state in society, and gain loyalty to the government.

The two species of monarchist philosophy fitted together closely. Mercantilist stratagems and "executive authority" could supply the political influence and power that would make of Wilson's prescriptions a reality. Wilson's scheme could legitimate the techniques of Hamilton and his spiritual brethren. Not surprisingly, the supporters of each philosophy often found themselves acting together and thinking alike.

That republican groups in the Convention found such schemes frightening in their implications is clear. Madison declared with some asperity, ". . . [we are] not trying to get a monarchy, [but] to prevent it . . ."[15] Benjamin Franklin observed "there is a natural inclination in mankind to Kingly Government. It sometimes relieves them of Aristocratic domination. They had rather have one tyrant than five hundred. It gives more of the appearance of equality among Citizens, and that they like."[16] Whether Franklin was speaking to both factions or not, the republican faction was aware that such "natural inclinations" existed and were important. For them, the corollary was different from that of Hamilton, Morris, Wilson and their allies: a government that "enlisted the passions" and, by fostering "positive liberties," became the patron of the poor was a deadly menace to constitutionalism. So they argued the necessity of building a government upon the virtues of the more elevated and patriotic citizenry. Their aim was to contrive a government that would be above "corruption" or factional interest—largely above "politics" as later generations of Americans know it.

The different views—monarchist and republican, the theory of a corporate political will against that of politically neutral patriotism—

---

[15] *Records*, Vol. II, p. 35.
[16] *Records*, Vol. I, p. 83.

were refracted in two issues: representation and the separation of powers. We turn now to the first of these.

Representation

Madison was the most effective spokesman for the republican view. It was he who provided the rationale for the republican remedies of sectional insulation, large constituencies, checks and balances, and a nonpolitical head magistrate. Madison also came nearest to providing a complete alternate theory of government, though on most particular points he was supported by other republicans. As a point from which to begin an examination of representation and of republican theory Madison's views are the most useful and pertinent.

The central concept of republican theory of representation was that of "dissociation," of disabling the "interested" and therefore, presumably, sinister, majority. Madison is sometimes spoken of as the author of the conception of a "conservative majority." To infer from this language that he approved of power for majorities (conservative or not) or even of an effectively organized public will is to misread him. He plainly said in Number Ten of *The Federalist* that the majority must "be rendered, by their number and local situation, *unable to concert* and carry into effect schemes for oppression."[17] "Isolated compartments," "enlarging the sphere," and "filtration"—the three remedies proposed by republicans and especially Madison—all would have one effect in common, their tendency to fragment the public will, either by dividing it into geographically isolated communities or by severing the vertical links of influence between faction and its representatives.

The point of Madison's scheme for "enlarging the sphere" of the electoral constituency was not only to defeat the "sinister" majority, but to do away with majorities themselves or with a connected political will among the populace. Madison made this point clear when he argued that "the fewer the distinct parties and interests," the greater the danger to the Commonwealth; the greater "the *variety of parties* and interests," the less the danger will be."[18] According to this argument, a majority party representing effectively a great number of interests would be an evil; fragmentation of the public will was the desirable state of affairs.

Federal arrangements supplemented the representative scheme. Diverse state interests acted as a natural check upon central government and as a device to insure against a concerted faction, especially if—as Madison argued—delegates from the states represented differing primary producer interests.[19] To this argument, Madison added another: that the

---

[17] Emphasis added.

[18] *The Federalist,* Number Ten. Emphasis added.

[19] Cf. Warren, *op. cit.*, p. 257; *Records,* Vol. III, p. 451; also Number Thirty-Seven of *The Federalist.*

"insulation" afforded by the "isolated compartments" of a federal system would prevent factions from spreading from one state to another. In *The Federalist* Number Ten Madison applies the strategy of insulation to political causes generally, not only revolutionary movements. He wrote:

> A religious sect may degenerate into a political faction in part of the Confederacy; but the variety of sects dispersed over the face of it must secure the national councils against any danger from that source. A rage for paper money, for an abolition of debts, for an equal division of property, or for any other wicked project will be less apt to pervade the whole body of the Union than a particular member of it . . .

The Madisonian device of "filtration" was aimed at the same objective of placing government above "faction." The delegation of power through representation itself was one way to "refine and enlarge the public views." By further establishing large constituencies, Madison argued, the suffrages of the citizen would be rendered more "free" (presumably from demagogues) and would "'be more likely to center in men who possess the most attractive merit and the most diffusive and established characters."[20] Large constituencies would put a high premium upon personal note and esteem among many cosmopolitan worthies.

Filtration was to be promoted also by another device: indirect election to the Senate. Some republicans proposed indirect election by the state legislatures; Madison originally proposed election by the House for it carried the principle of filtration one step farther, lengthening the distance between the Solons of the upper house and local faction. The Senate would, he argued, form a bulwark against future factional majorities, against a time when the dispossessed would "outnumber those who have been placed above the feelings of indigence."[21] For this reason, Madison also argued that the Senators should be men of wealth and have long terms of office.[22]

In the Convention the pure Madisonian strategy of encouraging rule by the patriotic political stratum had to yield to the small-state revolt and the New Jersey Plan. Madison, with Wilson, Hamilton, and other nationalists, was almost irreconcilable on the Connecticut Compromise and especially that part of it which called for a representation by states in the Senate. Yet he and other republicans eventually recognized that they got at least part of their loaf by "filtration" through state legislatures. Madison himself ultimately joined with Dickinson and other federalists to support the Compromise largely because he recognized this fact.[23]

The monarchist faction and more radical republicans offered Madison

---

[20] *The Federalist,* Number Ten.
[21] *Records,* Vol. I, p. 422.
[22] *Ibid.,* p. 423.
[23] *Ibid.,* pp. 152-53, 158; Warren, *op. cit.,* pp. 193-96.

and his allies a sharp and well-reasoned opposition. Essentially the quarrel was over representation—who and what should be represented and how to achieve that representation. At the root of the quarrel lay two opposing philosophies of politics and of the appropriate organization of the public will.

A striking feature of Madison's argument was the faith he put in men of "attractive merit" and "diffusive and established character." He did not acknowledge that the people might have as much to fear from worthy patriots as from outright demagogues or the rich. Madison suggested that wisdom and character in the personnel of government plus his "republican remedies" were the alpha and omega of good government. His discussions of representation implied an overriding purpose: to minimize the influence of faction and interest in the expectation that at least some men of great merit and inflexible civic devotion would rise to the top. To put the matter another way, he relied heavily upon patriotism to supply the spirit of government, and tried to dampen other influences. The monarchist faction took exception on several scores, all relating to a common theme: that talk of civic virtue or patriotism as the major principle or mainspring of government was not only nonsensical but dangerous.

One argument by Hamilton, Morris, King, and others was that a government not founded solidly on interest and made attractive to the able and ambitious through their desire for place and advantage would collapse because of the insubstantiality of the human passions upon which it rested. "It is a great mistake," said Mercer, "to suppose that the paper we are to propose will govern the United States. It is the men whom it will bring into the Government and their interest in maintaining it that is to govern them."[24] If the Constitution was to raise a great pyramid of federal government, they argued, it must have a solid base in ambition, interest, and common prejudice.[25] The Hamiltonian argument for turning interest to the side of government was supported at this point also by the insistence from Wilson and Mason upon carrying the democratic principle into the mass of the people and supporting a "popular pyramid" upon a broad base. Both groups, for their different reasons, found patriotism too pallid a prescription.

A second fear, shared by both monarchists and some radical democrats, was that so much high principle might well cover dirty business in practice. Gouverneur Morris, who warned against being "righteous overmuch or wise overmuch," flatly asserted a belief that a wealthy Senate or legislature, notwithstanding their patriotism, would oppress the mass of the people.[26] Hamilton expressed a similar conviction that the patriotic

---

[24] *Records*, Vol. II, p. 289.
[25] *Ibid.*, p. 52.
[26] *Ibid.*, p. 52.

zeal of a republic quickly wanes, leaving the political field to petty demagogues and corrupt "undertakers" (read, contractors, jobbers, and speculators).[27] For their part, the more radical republicans feared that what was being established was an aristocracy only slightly disguised by calling oligarchic devices "filtration" and "enlarging the spheres."[28] The point that both monarchist and radical had in common was the belief that a republican oligarchy could be as hardhearted and prejudiced as any other oligarchy.

The scheme for "enlarging the spheres" was also challenged by a number of delegates, including men like Gerry and Mason, but also Franklin, Wilson, and that doughty monarchist, Gouverneur Morris. It was Morris who went straight to the heart of the matter. If, he declared, the scheme of "enlarging the spheres" were meant for a nation of peasants, that would be one thing; but it is badly conceived for a future society of commerce, industry, and mechanics. "Let the rich mix with the poor," he said, "and in a commercial country they will establish an oligarchy."[29] Madison's "enlarged spheres," he argued, would only accentuate this tendency. "The schemes of the rich will be favored by the extent of the country. The people in such distant parts cannot communicate and act in concert. They will be dupes of those who have more knowledge and intercourse."[30]

Partly, those of decidedly monarchist persuasion, such as Morris and Hamilton, were pleading a case for their section and their friends. Certainly they were planning for and advancing a commercial, industrial, and urban society. Yet their views had a deeper philosophical basis that involved the nature of politics itself. They were arguing, in the face of rather pretentious and pious notions of republican virtue, that interest pervades politics. They were saying that interest is legitimate. They were saying that the way to protect interests is to give them frank recognition and a place in the representative and political scheme. For them the objective of a republican scheme was not that of winnowing patriots from the chaff, but giving play to interest, melding interest with interest, and building a powerful and just government by collecting diverse interests and prejudices into a program for the corporate good.

These differing philosophies of representation had specific practical consequences, especially for the House of Representatives and the Presidency. As a result of the Connecticut Compromise and earlier agreements in the Convention, representation in the Senate was no longer an open question. Representation was by states, the senators themselves to be elected by the state legislatures. But the election of the House and of the

---

[27] *Records,* Vol. I, pp. 287, 288.
[28] See, for example, Mason: *Records,* Vol. II, pp. 629 et. seq.
[29] *Records,* Vol. I, p. 512.
[30] *Ibid.,* p. 514.

President were still to be decided. The Compromise provided that the House should represent numbers: but how many for each representative? The Convention had earlier agreed that the President should be elected by Congress for seven years, and that provision had remained unchallenged for several weeks. As the Convention moved steadily toward definite and precise constitutional provisions, these questions—of a "numerous House" and the election of the President—were again sharply contested.

Debate over representation converged squarely and expectably on the size of constituencies. Given the local character of commercial and industrial enterprise of that day and the primitive state of communications, an effective representation of interests required a careful adjustment in the size of constituencies. The constituency was to the delegates an image of what government in the United States was to be. It should be neither so small that it would be politically lopsided or prey to the "vicious arts" of corruption and extreme demagogy, nor so huge that only a few could have an effective voice. From their differing perspectives both monarchist and radical argued this thesis, in opposition to Madison and the moderate republicans.

The groups that supported small constituencies and a numerous House did so for many reasons. Hamilton and Gouverneur Morris supported small constituencies because they only could achieve effective representation of economic interests, and derivatively a "virtual" representation of the people.[31] Hamilton especially argued in Convention and Number Thirty-Five of *The Federalist* that, far from destroying an effective representation of the "people," the welfare and the rights of the humbler classes would be most effectively protected through "virtual representation," through a kind of "syndical paternalism"[32] that would give an effective voice to their natural patrons: the greater merchant (or entrepreneur), landholders, and professionals.[33] However oligarchic the

---

[31] *Ibid.*, pp. 288, 308-309, 376, 381, 512.

[32] Richard Hofstadter, *The American Political Tradition* (New York: Alfred A. Knopf, 1948), p. 9.

[33] Hamilton's argument for "virtual representation" may seem disingenuous to the modern reader. Part of the thesis he was propounding, though, was important and substantially true: that the separate interests among the governing classes together with their common interest in governing could be effective levers for insuring responsiveness to the general good and to particular interests shared by them with parts of the wider populace. In particular, he was also arguing that devices designed primarily or only to get "good men" for government were not enough, but required to supplement them a representation of discrete and various interests. That we of a later period might well agree more with Hamilton than with Madison is patent. Granted social pluralism and modern economic conditions the constituency or the representative system that includes and gives effective voice to many interests, great and small, will probably better represent both the common good and the particular welfare than the constituency that gives voice only to Madison's common sentiment about who are virtuous representatives. In defense of Madison, the conditions were not those of "social pluralism and modern economic conditions."

intent of Hamilton and allies, that intent coincided in practical consequence with the objectives of radicals who wanted the representatives closely dependent upon the electorate. Also, Hamilton's proposals agreed with the views put forward by Wilson and backed by Pinckney and Franklin. For them, power and popularity went together and therefore, as Wilson argued, if a "popular pyramid" were to be raised, the scheme of representation had on the one hand to establish a like mind between the representative and his constituents, and also to reflect the diverse sentiments of right and common good held among the populace. The whole of the opposition to the strictly Madisonian scheme could meet on Hamilton's objection that the House of Representatives would be "on so narrow a scale as to warrant a jealousy in the people of their liberties."[34] The two monarchist factions were solidly agreed that the federal government should erect a frame of representation that would stimulate a corporate sentiment, either through mutual interest or collective democratic will. With their differing sentiments and philosophies, but with a common practical end, these diverse groups came together to form generally a common bloc opposed to the philosophy of "enlarging the spheres" and determined to limit the size of the constituencies.

The same alliance of monarchist, nationally-minded democrats and "states' rights" radicals figured in the provision for an independently elected president. The original Virginia Plan proposed an executive elected by the legislature (without making clear whether the executive was to be plural or singular). For radicals such as Gerry and Martin the scheme was obnoxious because it would produce "constant intrigue"[35] between the two branches and because it removed the executive too far from a local dependence.[36] Hamilton, Gouverneur Morris, and Wilson objected because the executive would be too narrowly based. Hamilton and Wilson especially argued for independent election, without the intervention of the states or the legislature.[37] Morris urged the removal of the seven-year restriction upon the term of office.[38] Their motives were, variously, fear of cabal, a desire for executive vigor, responsiveness to the "people," and a representation of the corporate whole. The two groups were able to agree upon a four-year term with no limit upon succession, independent election, and a college of electors appointed as the state legislatures "may direct."[39]

---

[34] *Records,* Vol. II, pp. 553-554.

[35] *Records,* Vol. I, p. 80; Vol. II, p. 105.

[36] Vol. II, p. 32.

[37] Wilson was the first to propose a single executive and independent election by an electoral college. *Records,* Vol. I, pp. 63, 71, 77. Hamilton also favored an electoral college. *Ibid.,* p. 272.

[38] *Ibid.,* Vol. II, p. 50.

[39] A principal reason for agreement was dislike of executive dependence on the legislature. "Cabal and faction" were the most frequently mentioned evils; but many also wanted government that was more popularly based and an executive more di-

The formula for the election of the President further limited the Madisonian scheme of representation and in a way similar to the provision for election of the House. Small constituencies for the House gave Congress a more popular base and made it also more representative of many groups. A wider and more inclusive representation was, similarly, provided for the Presidency. By destroying the dependence upon Congress, the electoral college rested presidential power at least partially (though indirectly) upon the people. It also provided in two ways for a representation of the whole: by making the President's constituency the whole nation; and by ensuring that the President would be responsive to sectional and local concerns.

The representative formula in the Constitution taken as a whole was, of course, a complex one. It set the size of the constituencies for the House of Representatives and the qualifications of the electors for that House by reference to the "most numerous branch" of the state legislatures.[40] It established equal representation of the states and per capita voting in the Senate. It included, finally, the electoral college mechanism for electing the President.

Today, living under different conditions, we can easily see that the representative plans of the various factions in the Convention did not ultimately have the consequences their proponents expected. Today, it is Madison's large constituency that more nearly promotes both "virtual" and inclusive representation, and the small constituencies that are often the "undemocratic" ones. The ways in which the great pyramid of representative power and authority is now sustained would have confounded both Wilson and Hamilton. Yet the delegates were wise in their understanding that the constituencies were the representative republic writ small and their philosophies of representation faced squarely the issue of what that representative republic was to be.

The delegates combined several philosophies of representation. They sought to achieve responsiveness to immediate and local concerns, an element of "virtual" representation, constituencies in which the voice of the cosmopolitan patriot would be effective, and representation of the corporate whole. At the same time, through representation, the delegates firmly connected the organization of central government with the politics of federalism.

---

rectly related to the people. At the same time, all the delegates feared that direct popular choice would lead to civil disorder and foreign influence. The electoral college was thus a reasonable compromise. According to Gouverneur Morris, the provision associating the state legislatures allayed some of the fears of the radicals and opened the way for unlimited succession. *Ibid.*, p. 501.

[40] The quota initially agreed upon in the Convention—one representative for each 40,000 inhabitants (as enumerated by formula) was not that which appeared in the Constitution. Washington moved and secured the adoption of the 30,000 quota on the last day of substantive business in Convention.

The formal representative provisions of the Constitution were central because of the absence of other political agencies, such as national political parties. The role these provisions have played in the whole constitutional scheme has been a distinctive feature of American politics. They were intended to supplement the popular will, to make it broadly representative and also responsive to many interests. They were also meant to strengthen the Republic and to provide a security against factious politics, sudden majorities, or the dominance of the whole of the polity by a part. The search for an acceptable compromise led toward the three principles of multiple modes of representation, inclusiveness, and formal provision to insure both. In the "politics" of the Convention the result was happy and possibly the pre-condition for a Constitution. For the American nation, the same principles restrain but also help to make tolerable our national party politics.

Separation of Powers

The political and philosophical differences between monarchist and republican over representation were extended by differences over the organization of the branches of the central government, especially the purposes and precise expression of the separation of powers. Everyone accepted as a matter of course the idea of the separation of powers. It was the familiar thing, engrained in their political habits and theories of government. At the same time the delegates had sharp theoretical differences parallelling the divisions over representation. Hamilton advocated a conception based upon British and Tory models. Similar views were held by those who, like Robert Morris, were interested in executive "efficiency," and by James Wilson and Pinckney who wanted the President to be a powerful popular symbol. Their ideals were similar to those of traditional monarchists, especially to such historic conceptions as that of a "patriot king." Madison and other republicans struck out more boldly, drawing upon a wider variety of historical sources and fundamental theory to fashion a distinctive American version of separation of powers.

The two factions differed over the purposes to be served by separation of powers as much as they did about arrangements. Monarchists wished to institute through separation of powers a compound of political influence and popular will that would serve the positive goal of promoting national strength and prosperity along with individual security. Madisonians and most republicans conceived of separation of powers primarily as a technique to dissociate institutions and check the accumulation of power or an irresponsible use of it. Either group would have accepted the other's purposes as having merit. Their differences were, in part, matters of degree. Yet in their whole conceptions of arrangements and the temper they sought to infuse into those arrangements, the two views were distinct.

Separation of powers, as expressed in the American Constitution, is an intricate arrangement. It includes both a "separation" as that term was traditionally understood and a set of "checks and balances." Briefly, the two houses, the President, and the courts are given a separate and an "independent" will. Yet the courts are checked by the presidential power over appointment and by the congressional authority to determine jurisdiction; the Congress is checked by the presidential powers of veto and of initiative in foreign policy and executive decision; the President is checked by the treaty and appointment clauses, by the powers to impeach and to override a veto; Congress and the President are checked by judicial review.

Because of the intricacy of the machinery, important differences of philosophy about separation of powers are often overlooked. The delegates in Convention, however, and particularly the republican and monarchist groups, articulated well the principles that ought to determine these arrangements. An examination of these philosophies is valuable to understanding separation of powers and the parts played by the separate "powers."

Basic differences about representation were expressed mainly on the size of constituencies for representatives; similarly an issue that brought out differences of fundamental constitutional theory in respect to separation of powers was the role contemplated for the Senate.

A strictly Madisonian rationale of "filtration" urged that the virtues the Senate should bring to government are wisdom and probity. Madison's argument ran: "The use of the Senate is to consist in its proceeding with more coolness, with more system, and with more wisdom, than the popular branch."[41] It should be as free from corruption as possible, and therefore, it ought not to be a numerous body. Madison proposed also that the Senate be elected by the House for nine years, one-third retiring every three years.[42] In his view, senators were "the impartial umpires and guardians of justice and general good." Republicans sometimes cited Roman examples when discussing separation of powers and the Senate; and the example of the Roman Senate, though not specifically a model for them, suggests particularly what some, at least, wanted the Senate to be: a body expressing virtue and wisdom and devoted to the permanent interests of the state.

The monarchist faction, especially Hamilton and Morris, put little faith in virtue or wisdom. For them, the Senate was important primarily for the temper and interests it represented: those of the propertied and aristocratic. Senators would be friends of the government and representative of the major interests within the Commonwealth. Not patriot zeal but their wealth and position would make them independent and

[41] *Records,* Vol. I, p. 151.
[42] *Ibid.,* pp. 151, 392, 423.

statesmanlike. Let them therefore, said Hamilton, be drawn from those having a "distinct, permanent share in the government." They will represent the wealthier few; the lower house the many citizens of modest circumstances. The first "will check the unsteadiness of the second."[43] Gouverneur Morris argued, further, that separate representation of the wealthy few would be desirable on two scores: it would enable the many to be more effectively represented on a separate basis, free from the influence of aristocratic patrons; and it would fix upon the wealthy few a square responsibility for the policies they supported.[44] He, and Hamilton with him, insisted that "aristocracy" was inevitable and even desirable. They both argued, though in distinct ways, that a failure to recognize the plain fact of differences in social advantage (and consequently political power) by confounding rich and poor together in one scheme of "republican" representation and government would lead to the oppression of the many. Essentially, they were saying, first, that the clash of interests between rich and poor and their differing political advantages should be openly recognized; and second, once recognized, these differences should be dealt with by a scheme that would protect both and win the loyalties of both to the government.

Hamilton and his like-minded friends did not argue that the Senate would be the "umpires and guardians of justice and general good." They were sensible that wealth corrupts and that ambition moves great men more than lesser ones. Most concurred with Gouverneur Morris that "wealth tends to corrupt the mind and nourish its love for power, and to stimulate it to oppression."[45] They were therefore prepared to concede that a large measure of popularity would be a necessity for the House of Representatives, not only to secure popular support and defend liberties (agreeing with Wilson, Mason, and Franklin), but as a just counterweight to the Senate. But conceding the first arrangement, then they argued that property and aristocracy would be requisite for the Senate. And granted acceptance of the first two propositions, then commanding power, influence, and prestige must reside in the executive. For only power and influence in the executive could ward off the tyranny of an aristocratic junto in the legislature.[46] On this point a number agreed with Hamilton and Morris. Wilson argued, in support of the same proposition, that even greater tyranny sprang from Parliament after the destruction of the power of the Crown in England.[47] With Madison, these men agreed on the "amazing violence and turbulence of the democratic spirit."[48] With him, they conceived an oligarchic second chamber. If,

[43] *Ibid.*, p. 299.
[44] *Ibid.*, pp. 511, 512.
[45] *Ibid.*, Vol. II, p. 52.
[46] *Records*, Vol. II, p. 284, 285.
[47] *Ibid.*, p. 301.
[48] *Records*, Vol. I, p. 389.

however, rich and poor could check each other, why then should there be legislative progress at all? And if there were no progress, whence confidence in the government? and to whom, in a world of growing privilege, ought the people to look for redress? Gouverneur Morris answered: "It is necessary . . . that the Executive Magistrate should be the guardian of the people, *even of the lower classes,* against Legislative tyranny, against the great and wealthy who in the course of things will necessarily compose—the Legislative body."[49]

Without agreeing with the scheme for an oligarchic Senate, Pinckney, the two Morrises, Franklin, Wilson and others were sympathetic to the Hamiltonian argument for popularity in the House matched by presidential independence and even a measure of popular dictatorship. Their differences were largely over means and degree.

The monarchist faction wished to make the executive a powerful *political* agency in its own right. They did not blush to say that a President would and ought to be moved by ambition and love of fame.[50] Accordingly, they wished him to be independent of the legislature and have (or represent) a national constituency of his own, opposing especially the Madisonian program for a legislative election. They were jealous of the executive veto and the role of the Senate in appointments. They wanted the Senate to be an "arsenal of statesmen" and the Council, if there were to be one, a body that would do the President's will and enhance his prestige. Their objective was "energy" in the executive to make the influence of the government felt and to give the citizens a lively sense of the mingling of its interests with theirs.[51] For some, like Wilson, that aim meant primarily some formula for the popular election of the President. For others, like Hamilton and the two Morrises, that aim dictated as well "influence" and patronage, and an executive that would be a vast establishment unto itself, headed by a chief magistrate who was both the director of civil and military officers and the political chief of the nation.[52]

The monarchist scheme at its purest was unacceptable to the delegates, and for good reason, since it would obviously tend toward corruption, an engrossment of the powers of the Senate by the President, popular dictatorship in government and clientelism among the citizenry. Yet some points put forward by the monarchists are worth attention.

---

[49] *Ibid.,* Vol. II, p. 52. Emphasis added.

[50] See, for example, the debates over the term of the President: *Records,* Vol. II, pp. 53-103; *passim;* on other points, see pp. 242-301; 501-539.

[51] Cf. Records, Vol. I, pp. 284-289; also Number Twenty-Seven of *The Federalist.*

[52] This objective suggests why appointment of legislators to executive office was so hotly disputed in the Convention. For those of an extreme Hamiltonian persuasion this issue was the crux of the debate over the relations between the legislature and the President. Without influence, the executive would be impotent. With it, he would be armed to work for the common weal, even if his work had to be carried on over the heads of a legislative "oligarchy."

They assumed that the problem was one of giving the power to act for the common good. They argued, further, that government is channeled properly not by dividing and weakening it, but by insuring that countervailing influences are heard in the national councils and given an effective voice by adequate grants of political power. That there should be a broad representative foundation to the government the monarchist accepted, for without it no great structure could be reared. That broad and popular influence should be steadied by a stable oligarchy. But against both of these must be a force able to speak for and take initiative for the common good. In this scheme, a powerful tension between the principles of democracy, plutocracy, and monarchy drives the representatives of each to claim power for the common good, and thereby to extend and popularize the political principles upon which they stand.[53]

The republican assumption was that the Presidency should not be a political office. The republican agreed with the monarchist that the executive should be both strong and responsible. There the identity of program ended. In what, or how, was the President to be strong and responsible? Madison in particular, and with him Mason and others, relied in the first instance upon the President's *personal* merit.[54] He was to be made independent; but he was also to be denied the *political* weapon of influence, and even to some extent of appointment.[55] Madison agreed that the executive was the "naturally weaker," requiring special constitutional aids. Because the republicans feared abuses from a popular executive, however, they preferred not to augment the political power of the Presidency to match the potential of a more powerful legislature. Instead, they wanted to distribute powers carefully *between* the branches to assure their independence. Enumeration, a qualified veto, impeachment, and sharing powers with the Senate have together this tendency: to balance the two houses and the executive without adding to the total quantum of political power exercised by legislature or executive, either in concert or separately.

For political energy, the republican depended upon disinterested patriotism and the influence that a cosmopolitan elite could bring to the support of any issue. Madison perceived that the influence of such a stratum would be essential to sustain republican government. But patriotism is not enough to provide for the politics of a diverse and changing nation.

The effect of the republican solution would be not only to neutralize

---

[53] Notice that the tension between democracy, plutocracy, and monarchy is also an application, in an eighteenth century context, of the ancient Greek and Roman theme of the balanced or mixed constitution.

[54] *Records*, Vol. I, pp. 138-39; Vol. II, pp. 31, 32, 56, 57.

[55] Eg., the initial suggestion that two-thirds of the Senate should advise and consent on appointments as well as treaties. *Ibid.*, Vol. II, pp. 42, 43.

the executive but to eliminate most of politics from the major issues of government. By implication, a major policy issue would not be a test of political forces but a clash of magistrates. Such a struggle would be "political" in the sense that it would involve personalities and ideals of public policy. But the struggle would lack a political solution, for by the nature of the case the important interests would not be engaged, nor active in the solution, nor responsible for its execution. Qualitative political changes, responsive to deep trends of social evolution, would pose a great if not irremedial difficulty for the Madisonian prescription, for a transition to a new constitutional position through the growth in relative power of one branch of government was precluded. Hamilton and Morris, and others such as Wilson, argued that the particular branches would be, in fact and despite any constitutional theory, political agencies. They said therefore that the paths along which an orderly expansion could take place should be marked out. They suggested that corruption and even cabal and interested faction might have their uses in supplying viable modes for the growth of constitutional power. Joined with the philosophy of the "popular pyramid," the monarchist views had much to commend them, especially for later generations; the republican philosophy was, by comparison, rigid and somewhat parochial. It also trusted much to a formal machinery designed to insure honest and prudent government mainly by banishing politics from government.

Fearing politics and the interested majority, the republican faction also distrusted proposals designed to make government an active partner in expanding economic opportunity. Carefully they confined and fragmented the public will to keep the people safe from the temptations of political spoils. Their ideals for central government were the fair adjudication of interests and the executive leadership of honest, devoted public servants. For a nation of increasing wealth and diversity, that ideal could only prove ultimately sterile. For in eschewing politics, the republicans thrust aside the conception that the government should and must act positively in the greater common interest. They rejected policies that might serve to moderate inequalities by putting men on a new, common footing and increased prosperity for all.[56] That philosophy, translated into political reality, would not be pleasant to contemplate: a government that would leave each man as it found him and declare its neutrality in the issues of riches and poverty, all the while supposing the result to be good because patriots in national office piously declared it to be so.

Separation of powers and the distribution of powers among President and Congress in the Constitution did not wholly express either of these

[56] Madison faced these implications squarely in declaring a primary function of the Senate to form a bulwark against future factional majorities in a time when the dispossessed would "outnumber those who have been placed above the feelings of indigence." *Records,* Vol. I, p. 243.

philosophies, nor even a compromise between them, but carefully and sanely reconciled them in a scheme of government in which the parts could work together. The independently elected President, the electoral college, and the more numerous House were concessions to the democratic views. The clearest examples of monarchical influence are found in the veto, the strong appointive power, and the absence of a provision limiting presidential succession. The handiwork of Madison and the republicans appear in the restrictions upon the popular and monarchical principles, in the provision for the participation of the Senate in the exercise of the presidential power, and in the whole array of intricate checks and balances designed not only to curb power but also to rationalize its use.

To our present benefit, the monarchist component was firmly entrenched. The Constitution did ultimately lend itself to positive political aims; the President emerged as a popular chief; a politics of nationwide interests succeeded the politics of sectionalism. To our benefit, oligarchy has been matched by an increasingly powerful democracy, and inequality of condition by expanding opportunity. The vision of men like Hamilton, Morris, and Wilson of a thriving, corporate polity broadly based upon interest and an organized public will was vindicated.

Equally to our benefit, however, the Hamiltons, Wilsons, and Morrises did not entirely prevail. In the theory of a "popular pyramid" was much of the flavor of popular dictatorship, and perhaps even of a reign of virtue. Hamilton's programs had a cynical tone of *enrichissez vous* in respect to the separate interests and classes of society, and they also smacked of fraud and rank corruption in respect to politics. Both schemes were, as Robert Yates wryly commented, "very remote from the idea of the people."[57]

Madison, especially, understood many of the dangers lying in the direction of monarchist policy. He saw clearly the less benign aspects of American politics: the fetishes and petty jealousies of factions and groups, the tug of sectionalism, the latent militarism in American sentiments, and a hankering for demagogues and for symbolic victories in politics. Republican government, he believed, rested upon a compact of republicans. If that compact was to last, it had to be somewhat removed from politics. The men without party or king, the disinterested patriots and defenders of the contract, were for him the vital political stratum upon which the constitution depended. They would defend the constitutional temper of politics.[58] They would defend the union and act to bridge the gulf among factions, sections, and regions. For the sake of the Constitution and the Union, Madison argued, do not destroy that saving leaven.

[57] *Records,* Vol. I, p. 301.

[58] For a modern statement of this theme, see V. O. Key, Jr., *Public Opinion and American Democracy* (New York: Alfred A. Knopf, 1960), especially Ch. 21.

The delegates saw both the dangers of the opposing philosophies and their indispensible merit. Government is a trust for the common good. Free government requires that leaders be steadfast in republican virtue: that they honor and strengthen that covenant made among themselves and with the people. Progress toward an enlarged common good is equally an end of popular government. It requires leadership and, at times, large acts of sovereignty. In a short phrase, some must be for the king just as some must be for the contract of government. The Founding Fathers were conscious of that fact. But they also saw more deeply: that these loyalties had to be reconciled between citizens themselves and within government itself.

Chapter VI

A GOVERNMENT OF LAWS

The central and most commonly acknowledged purpose of a constitution, for eighteenth-century Americans, was to secure a "government of laws, not of men." What people meant by that phrase differed, as we shall see, yet it was almost universally held that government rested upon law, law possessed by the separate members in society and protecting their liberty and property. The society was "law-ridden," as one author has phrased it, a description that carries two meanings. People treasured the law and legal modes of settlement. At that time, also, American society was in that stage of legal evolution in which the common law and the judiciary played an enormous role in settling disputes and supervising governmental and private organizations in the society.[1] Although the legal heritage of the Americans, deriving from Elizabethan England and the Puritan Revolution, from the reign of George III, and from their own experience, included both authoritarian and libertarian precepts,[2] that heritage nevertheless boasted a dominant common theme. Government,

[1] Roscoe Pound, *The Spirit of the Common Law* (Boston: Marshall Jones Company, 1921); George L. Haskins, *Law and Authority in Early Massachusetts* (New York: The Macmillan Company, 1960); Barck and Lefler, *Colonial America* (New York: The Macmillan Company, 1958), Ch. 15. Cf. also William Blackstone, *Commentaries on the Laws of England.*

[2] Edward S. Corwin, *The "Higher Law" Background of American Constitutional Law* (Ithaca: Cornell University Press, 1957), pp. 84 ff. Cf. also William Holdsworth, *A History of English Law* (London: Methuen and Company, 1938), Vol. X.

though deriving its just powers from the consent of the governed, could not derogate fundamental right. Positive government was only a lesser part of a greater body of law; it rested upon a wider, more ancient foundation.[3]

This tradition of fundamental antecedent right was not faithfully reflected in the Convention. Only a handful of the delegates argued for a Bill of Rights. Various authors have commented upon the scant attention given to the fundamental institution of judicial review.[4] The debates in the Convention showed a primary concern with establishing a government rather than with securing protections of liberty. Critics of the Convention argue that the delegates' scheduling of political priorities also reflected their true sympathies in matters of fundamental liberties and the rule of law. Two considerations, however, somewhat mitigate the force of such a criticism.

The American heritage of common law and constitutional tradition was ambiguous. By "rule of law," some meant fundamental liberties and the common law, others a judicial attitude in governmental decision, still others the legal authority of the Constitution itself. With respect to the rule of law, the delegates had to compromise, as they did on the nature of the union and the organization of central government. But compromises relating to the rule of law were approached more indirectly, however, than the others; and they appeared mainly as parts of or amendments to other arrangements. Radical republicans and the stricter "federalists" of the Convention especially made their mark here.[5] Though they had little positive theory of government to advance—after the defeat of the New Jersey Plan and the Connecticut Compromise—they argued and bargained doggedly to secure concessions for what they thought were constitutionalism and the rule of law. Against their point of view the Madisonian stands out most distinctly; and the resulting constitutional theory of the rule of law may be fairly accurately represented as a synthesis of the two.

A second major consideration is that the delegates were prone to view the rule of law as something that pertained to the whole system of

[3] Note here the pertinence of the Ninth and Tenth Amendments: "The enumeration in the Constitution, of certain rights, shall not be construed to deny or disparage *others retained by the people.*" And "The powers not delegated to the United States by the Constitution, nor prohibited by it to the States, are reserved to the States respectively, *or to the people.*" (Emphasis added.) See Corwin, *op. cit.*, pp. 8, 9. McLaughlin observes that in the case of Massachusetts, the Bill of Rights *preceded* the rest of the constitution. Andrew C. McLaughlin, *A Constitutional History of the United States* (New York: D. Appleton-Century Company, 1935), p. 115,

[4] For instance, Charles Warren, *The Making of the Constitution* (Boston: Little, Brown and Company, 1928), p. 531; Max Farrand, *The Framing of the Constitution of the United States* (New Haven: Yale University Press, 1913), p. 154.

[5] The most important members of these groups were Gerry, Martin, Dickinson, Ellsworth, Johnson, and Sherman. They were joined on some issues by Carroll, Charles Pinckney, Franklin, Randolph, and Rutledge.

government, secured by all its arrangements. We today associate the "rule of law" principally with the guarantee of fundamental rights, of due process, and of the final jurisdiction of the courts. For us, in the words of Charles Pinckney, judicial review and the federal judiciary form the "keystone of the arch."[6] The political theory of the delegates was more profound. Separation of powers, the representative system (and especially the place of the Senate), the distribution of powers between the Union and the states, were for them as important as the more specifically judicial arrangements. The former supported, made possible, the lawful spirit in government and the citizen that alone could make legal arbitration tolerable. The delegates did not ignore the problem of liberty or of securing a rule of law; they conceived the problem more widely than we today are wont to do.

The Lawful Temper

The problems that confronted the delegates in securing a government of laws were rooted in the basic dilemmas created by the "disharmonious society." In the issue of fundamental constitutionalism, as in those of federal union and the organization of the public will, the delegates agreed on the dangers of consolidation or dictatorship at one extreme, disunion and anarchy at another. They disagreed about how best to provide against the dangers, and what values, beyond a mere security, they ought to seek.

Men like Hamilton and Robert and Gouverneur Morris, as might be expected, were not particularly exercised over the subject. Though Hamilton, contrary to popular impression, did not oppose protections such as a Bill of Rights, he felt that their influence, whether good or bad, would be small. The loquacious Gouverneur Morris spoke little on the subject, and the silent Robert Morris did not speak at all. Their view of government did not attribute an important position to the concept of the rule of law. For them, the purpose of a constitution was to generate power and to channel it, but they showed scant interest in provisions to limit government other than the enumeration of its powers.

James Wilson, who otherwise seemed generally to stand for the cause of a national democracy, also showed a remarkable insensitivity to this issue of a government of laws. Like Madison and Pinckney, he argued strongly for federal laws acting directly upon the citizen, especially because he wanted a general body of federal law to make men conscious of their national citizenship and to give that citizenship legal expression. However, he largely ignored the issue of constitutional protections of

[6] In commending the Article on the Judiciary to the South Carolina Convention, Pinckney said: "under a wise management, this department might be made the keystone of the arch, the means of connecting and binding the whole together, of preserving uniformity in all the judicial proceedings of the Union . . ." Elliott, Vol. IV, p. 258.

liberty. For him, the security of the system lay in a mixture of democracy, monarchy, and aristocracy; the citizen's rights were made secure by federal vigor. When pressed on the issue of rights in the Pennsylvania ratifying convention, he said baldly that he regarded a Bill of Rights as unnecessary, that he had little sympathy with protections for specific liberties such as "liberty of the press."[7]

To understand the concept of rule of law in the Constitution, Madison's views are central. He of all the delegates probably had the clearest sense of what he wished to accomplish, and his contribution was unique in American constitutional theory.

Madison believed that a constitution ought primarily to protect that spirit of neutrality and probity upon which both common rights and a public will must rest. His schemes were aimed, first, at moderating "politics" and the spirit of faction by creating a judicial attitude in political decision: by delegating some substantially political matters to the agency of the courts, and by providing for participation of the judiciary in political decision. Second, he aimed at insulating the spirit of the laws, or the temper of constitutionality and lawfulness, from faction or immediate political interest. In his thinking, these two central objectives were related and yet distinct.

As elaborated in the Virginia Plan and in convention debate, Madison's scheme involved in the first instance the removal of the "most fruitful sources of discord" from decision by the states. He therefore argued for a federal judiciary to secure common rights throughout the states and to remove the issue of equal privileges and immunities from local decision. To protect foreign and interstate commerce, the substance of federal laws and treaties, and common republican principles throughout the whole of the United States, he insisted further upon a direct legislative veto over obnoxious laws passed in the states. And to preserve a judicial attitude in central government, he proposed not only "filtration" and the securing of "wisdom and probity" in the Senate, but a Council of Revision[8] to join the judiciary with the President and Senate in the framing and revision of legislation.

Madison's scheme of "judicializing" politics did not sit well with the delegates, partly because they appear to have misunderstood its import.

---

[7] Elliott, Vol. II, pp. 436, 449-50. In regard to such protections as "liberty of the press," many would have agreed with Wilson. Newspapers at that time were often libelous and usually close and unscrupulous advocates of some particular faction.

[8] The "Council of Revision" was a Madisonian enthusiasm. Other delegates were in favor of a "council," similar to the Governors' Councils or the English Privy Council of colonial times, that would both support and check the executive. Delegates differed over the composition of such a council, some wishing to include the heads of the most important executive departments, others wanting to include as well the leading officers of the two legislative houses and the Chief Justice of the Supreme Court. Madison urged particularly the inclusion of judicial officers; and he wanted to give the council a role in advising on laws and in the use of the executive veto.

Annexing the judges and a Council of Revision to the political process smacked too much of the rule of governor's councils and central court judges familiar in colonial times. That system and the role of the English Privy Council under the British system signified to the delegates not a government of laws, but that justice would put her sword to the use of the governors.[9]

Close inspection of Madison's plan suggests that his intention was different, especially since he did not make the judiciary but rather the Congress the supervisor of state legislation. Obviously, he was also interested in the judiciary not as an *aid to government,* but as an influence that would temper faction and improve legislation and government by expanding the *jurisdiction* in which the judicial attitude and the lawful spirit would be decisive or contributory. Madison's proposal for a Council of Revision did not survive in the Constitution itself, and Madison himself did not seem to care intensely that it did not. A wide *jurisdiction* for the judicial spirit was important to him not only for what it contributed to politics, but as a way in which to resolve those "most fruitful sources of discord." The fundamental philosophy that lay behind his suggestion did survive, however. The importance of that philosophy can be seen today in the state governments,[10] in the boards and commissions of the American political scene, in the regulatory process, and in the treatment of such "fruitful sources of discord" as interstate commerce.

If Madison was insistent upon a wide jurisdiction for the judicial attitude in American politics, he was doubly insistent that that jurisdiction be protected from the spirit of faction. Like other constitutionalists, he was concerned that that which pertained to the public not be made a private property, that the treasury or the fisc not be a gift in the keeping of a faction. But in his desire to place the spirit of the laws above faction, Madison understood one fundamental of republican philosophy with a direct and sharp vision that had no precedent. So far as the real foundations of the political contract are concerned, he argued, the government must be impartial and formally correct. That condition requires, of course, that the spirit of lawfulness and of due process be directly sought and promoted. But a second and perhaps even more important side of the proposition is the need for the deliberate protection of that spirit from faction. If a faction can use the laws as a club to overcome its enemies, then the contract is undone in two ways. Rights are invaded, which is a direct evil. A greater evil is that the *res publica* itself—the common sense of lawfulness and of the government as standing for that sense, protecting and enhancing it—is attacked at its foundation. That upon which the

---

[9] See, particularly, Warren, *op. cit.,* pp. 179, 646; *Records,* Vol. I, 81-84, 86; Barck and Lefler, *op. cit.,* Ch. 15.

[10] Particularly in their relation to subordinate agencies of state government.

whole depends is undermined, and by a contagious example that leads quickly to a destructive group warfare.

Madison, in arguing for a political will that was *public* and *judicially correct,* was supplying an emphasis that has been unique to American politics. The stamp of his mind and philosophy can be seen particularly in those categories of constitutional law where we use the term "public." Thus, when we say that taxation must be for a *public* purpose, that property can be condemned only for a *public* use, that the police power must serve the *public* benefit, we echo in part Madison's principle that the state not lend itself to faction.[11] Similarly with the delegation of legislative power.[12] Even in matters of fundamental liberties we have at heart one interest that is Madisonian: preventing the laws and the force of the state from use by one faction to persecute another.[13]

Judicial Review

However fundamental Madison's contribution may have been, his conception was both incomplete and flawed, as the more radical republicans were quick to declare. Men like Gerry, Martin, and Mason were, in the first instance, reluctant to see any primary powers of government removed from the local communities, even those "most fruitful sources of discord"; they were doubly opposed to a scheme that would give jurisdiction over those powers to a distant Congress. They distrusted Madison's "republican elite." Madison's plan appeared likely to support both the continuing accumulation of powers by the national government and the consolidation of those powers into a tyrannical system approaching dictatorial rule. Some of their critique seems today little better than a stubborn, carping negativism. In part their fears were mistaken and sometimes misplaced. Nevertheless, mistaken or not, they mounted an attack upon the Madisonian philosophy that was at times direct and radical, at times dogged and pragmatic, but in any event not to be gainsaid. From that dialectic came the principles of rule of law and judicial review as we know them today in the United States.[14]

---

[11] See especially, *Association of American Law Schools: Selected Essays on Constitutional Law* (Chicago: Foundation Press, 1938), Bk. I, Ch. 2; Bk. II, Chs. 3-5; Bk. IV, Ch. 2; Bk. V., Ch. 1.

[12] The doctrine of delegation of legislative power does not have anywhere else the peculiar import that it does in the United States. For a commentary, see *Ibid.*, Bk. IV, Ch. 2, Sec. 2; Vol. IV, pp. 219-251, "The Delegation of Legislative Power—The Limits of Discretion in Rule-Making," and Louis L. Jaffe, "Law Making by Private Groups," *Harvard Law Review,* Vol. 51 (1938), p. 201.

[13] An example is the "separation of church and state" imposed by the First Amendment: Congress may make no law respecting an "establishment of religion." Part of the effect of this clause is to protect individual liberty; it also serves to prevent contagious and destructive conflict that would undermine the constitutional temper in society. See, especially, Leo C. Pfeffer, *Church, State and Freedom* (Boston: Beacon Press, 1953).

[14] Madison did, in fact, show himself notably insensitive to precisely those dangers and the need for constitutional guarantees that had exercised this group. He saw

One institutional arrangement that occasioned protracted debate was the veto over unconstitutional state actions. Generally the delegates accepted the proposition that some kind of negative was needed. Yet from the opening days of the Convention they had argued whether that negative should be by executive force, by legislative action, or by court review.[15] In keeping with earlier schemes for amending the Articles, the delegates agreed that the executive should have the power "to call forth the force of the union"; but this provision answered only to an execution of federal laws. It would be of use for a clear case of insurrection or flagrant and direct defiance of the laws by a faction or small group of rebels. Could it be used to coerce a state? Most of the delegates thought not; and in any event they recoiled from the prospect. Also they sensed that such a provision would be of little use except where force was called forth by a resort to force: it was of no help for resistance that was less blatant and more insidious, and for that reason even more dangerous.

Madison's plan called for an oath by the state judges to uphold the Constitution; it also asked for a congressional veto of obnoxious state laws. In the original plan of the Randolph Resolutions, his expedient would have seemed appropriate, for in that plan the organs of government were outlined roughly and their powers not explicitly detailed or precisely limited. As the constitutional plan developed, however, and especially after the Connecticut Compromise, Madison's proposal appeared to be both too weak and too strong. The scheme was too weak, Wilson and Pinckney argued, because it did not firmly secure federal rights to the citizen. It was too strong because it involved the veto of a political body over the states and the general capacity of Congress to legislate where the states were "incompetent." Even Gouverneur Morris thought that such a power would be "terrible to the states," and argued that their traditional powers of police ought to be preserved intact.[16] Where Morris was perturbed, Gerry, Martin, Sherman, and Dickinson were scandalized. They were alarmed at so radical a redistribution of powers. They argued that the veto was unnecessary. They saw also a domination of the small states by the large and the possibility of political and perhaps even armed conflict.[17]

---

little use for a Bill of Rights, and when it was passed said only that it was "neither improper nor altogether useless" (*Records*, Vol. III, p. 357). He regarded the "general welfare" and "necessary and proper" clauses as merely declaratory and stated that they would be unlikely to provide a path for constitutional expansion. Similarly, he thought the enumeration of constitutional powers an adequate protection against misrule or tyranny. Subsequent history, the political sociology of his times, and, specifically, Hamilton's chancellorship under Washington show how much substance there was to the complaints of the radicals.

[15] Warren, *op. cit.*, p. 167; *Records*, Vol. I, pp. 52-54.

[16] *Ibid.*, p. 315; Also, *Creation of the Federal Judiciary*, Senate Document Number 91, Seventy-Fifth Congress, First Session (Washington: Government Printing Office, 1938).

[17] Warren, *op. cit.*, pp. 315-22; *Records*, Vol. II, pp. 26-28.

Several alternate formulae were tried and each secured some support, though they failed to appease the radical republicans. An even more extreme version that would allow Congress to legislate for the sake of the "general interest" or where the "harmony of the United States" might be "interrupted"[18] was adopted but immediately gave rise to objection. Randolph suggested a compromise that would allow the states to appeal to the national judiciary against a negative. As the proposals grew more cumbersome and less satisfactory, the Convention reversed its earlier action and rejected the whole scheme for a legislative veto. Finally, the delegates turned toward the judicial veto which Luther Martin and other radical republicans had favored from the beginning. That formula, taken originally by Martin from the New Jersey Plan, provided that:

> The Acts of the Legislature of the United States made in pursuance of this Constitution, and all treaties made under the authority of the United States, shall be the supreme law of the several States, and of their citizens and inhabitants; and the judges of the several States shall be bound thereby in their decisions; anything in the Constitutions and laws of the several states to the contrary notwithstanding.[19]

Apparently the delegates assumed also that they were committing themselves to a general formula of judicial review. Their subsequent debates over the Council of Revision and the Supreme Court indicate that they did. When the Committee on Style reported the final draft they changed the opening line of Martin's resolution to read "*This Constitution* and the laws of the United States which shall be made in pursuance thereof . . ."[20] As Martin indicated in a letter to the Maryland legislature, the provision as adopted contemplated not only a judicial negative upon the state laws and *constitutions,* but on the acts of Congress and the President as well.[21]

That this formula was adopted without dissent invites some attention, for many of the issues it touched upon were fundamental to particular factions within the Convention. The simple explanation would seem to be that the principal groups of partisans in the debate over this clause got what they wanted. Indeed, the clause was one of those rare constitutional formulae that gave the various groups not only what they wanted but probably more than they asked and in a better way. Pinckney, Wilson, and the nationalist group were satisfied, for the clause guaranteed the rights of federal citizenship. Gerry, Martin, Dickinson, and Rutledge were also content. The provision would control "force bills" and paper money emissions in the states. But it also provided for a milder form of coercion, avoiding either executive force or legislative political dictation,

---

[18] Warren, *op. cit.,* p. 314.

[19] *Records,* Vol. II, pp. 28-29; Warren, *op. cit.,* p. 319.

[20] Emphasis added.

[21] Warren, *op. cit.,* p. 320; *Records,* Vol. II, pp. 76-77; Elliott, Vol. I, p. 380.

and allowing the states to retain their traditional powers and exercise them flexibly.[22] Even Madison recognized this formula as better than his own.[23] On the one hand, it would give a wide, possibly an even wider, jurisdiction to judicial influence. Also, judicial review filled a gap in Madisonian thought: the problem of what agency should resolve the differences arising from those "most fruitful sources of discord." The judiciary could ably serve this purpose for at least some differences, a point that Madison recognized especially with respect to the power over commerce.[24] The same logic could be and was extended to other issues, such as controversies between the states, and rights under treaties.

The amicable harmony achieved in the Convention over the issue of a negative upon the states and the exercise of judicial review did not extend, however, to the position of the judiciary and to the *mode* of exercise of judicial review. The primary bone of contention was the Council of Revision. Madison and one or two allies such as Wilson continued stubbornly to push for the institution, especially because of the "good [that] would proceed from the perspicuity, the conciseness, and the systematic character which the code of laws would receive from the Judiciary talents."[25] They were apparently interested also in tempering and limiting the power of the legislature. On the first score, especially, they were opposed stoutly by the familiar group: Martin, Gerry, Dickinson, Sherman, Ellsworth, and several others representing small states and the more radical republican sentiments. The root of the opposition went deep. It took the form of a quarrel over separation of powers and the "independence" of the various branches, especially the judiciary. It raised also questions of the appointment of the judiciary, their tenure, and the scope of the judicial power. But the central theme was simple: the inflexible hostility of the radical republican to a "consolidation" of powers, to a mixing of executive, judicial, and legislative organs that by confusing and lumping powers would invite an unchecked accumulation of power or an irresponsible use of it. From British history, from colonial experience, and from their own state governments, they knew the dangers inherent in "councils" and in the close association of courts and executive. They were determined to have no such pattern of power in the Federal system.

Elbridge Gerry of Massachusetts and Luther Martin of Maryland

---

[22] On the significance of this last point, see Louis L. Jaffe, "Standing to Secure Review: Public Actions" *Harvard Law Review,* Vol. 74 (1961), pp. 1265-92. Professor Jaffe contrasts favorably the American technique of legal control of local and state governments with the bureaucratic (administrative) system of controls common to England and most of the Continent.

[23] Andrew C. McLaughlin, *The Confederation and the Constitution* (New York and London: Harper and Brothers Publishers, 1905), pp. 244-45.

[24] Warren, *op. cit.,* p. 560; Elliott, Vol. III, pp. 531-33; *Records,* Vol. II, pp. 440-42.

[25] *Madison's Papers* (Washington: Government Printing Office, 1848), Vol. II, p. 810.

took the lead in opposing a Council of Revision and in so doing left their lasting mark upon our judicial institutions.[26] Gerry argued that a Council was superfluous to judicial independence and that it would involve the judges in a conflict of interest between their roles as judges and legislators.[27] He argued that the Legislature and not the judges were the best guardians of the rights of the people.[28] He, with Martin, argued that the Council of Revision would either become a Privy Council on the English model or would speed the perversion of the Senate into such an institution. Finally, he said directly to Madison that he would rather have an executive veto than the confusion of powers entailed in the scheme of a Council.[29]

Gerry and his friends were making the arguments familiar today as the rationale for judicial self-restraint. Their arguments appear to have consolidated a group and gradually to have won over such key figures as Pinckney, Rutledge, Randolph, and Dickinson. The plan for a Council was almost entirely abandoned, surviving in the Constitution only in the provision that the President "may require the Opinion . . . of the principal officers in the executive Departments."[30] The Convention rejected any judicial role in legislation and went further to disapprove even of advisory opinions. They also abandoned a judicial power of impeachment in the interest of making the judicial power strictly independent and judicial.

We need not argue in detail the essential contribution both of the Madisonian philosophy and of the more radical republicans to the institution of judicial review and to a "government of laws." Madison, especially concerned with the republican stratum that would support a constitution and with the need for securing the judicial temper from destruction by faction, supplied the political elements of the formula. Gerry and his allies effectively limited this prescription and promoted those compromises that paved the way both for judicial review of a substantial scope and also for the acceptance of an important constitutional role of the federal judiciary.

Government of Limited Powers

To leave the discussion at this point would be to miss one of the essential contributions of the radical republicans and to do less than

---

[26] Gerry seems to have been the leading spirit, certainly the most tenacious and consistent.

[27] Pinckney stated the theme picturesquely. The Council, he said, would "involve them [the judiciary] in parties and give a previous tincture to their opinions." *Creation of the Federal Judiciary*, op. cit., p. 30.

[28] Also, Luther Martin: "A knowledge of mankind, and of Legislative affairs, cannot be presumed to belong in a higher degree to the Judges than to the Legislature." *Records*, Vol. II, p. 76.

[29] *Records*, Vol. II, p. 78.

[30] Article II, Paragraph 2, Clause 2.

justice to the spirit that animated them. Their quarrel over the judiciary and their demand for its independence and dissociation was rooted in a philosophy hostile both to the *accumulation* of power and to its *consolidation* in one mass. For this reason they stood as they did on the judiciary. They also distrusted the President, fought the veto, and resisted executive appointment of legislative members to positions in the administration. They wanted an independent Senate, conceiving it as a protection to the smaller states and as a political barrier securing the rights of the citizens. And for much the same reasons, most of this group were "small constituency" men on the issue of representation in the House of Representatives.

Their sentiment has been variously interpreted as a crabbed mistrust of power[31] or as a love of sturdy "grass-roots" democracy.[32] What differs sharply from either of these, however, was their desire to provide for formal external checks on political and administrative power, and on the tendency of government toward a sinister cohesion among officeholders, magistrates, and politicians. Where Madison feared faction, they feared both cabal and faction. Where Hamilton feared disorder, they argued that a measure of disorder was small price to pay for the guarantees of liberty and the continuing assurances that constitutional checks upon government were being defended and preserved. Where others argued for a broad power of government to benefit the populace, they insisted upon self-denying ordinances, rejecting proposals for a federal incorporation act, for banks and canals, national universities, and various other forms of sponsorship for particular groups.[33] They feared both the power and the blandishments of government. In large measure, theirs *was* a negative philosophy of government. Their philosophy of dissociation and independence, carried to the extremes they urged, would have made government itself unworkable. The central portion of their philosophy that survived in the Constitution has, however, stood the test of time and may have served the country well.

In the state ratifying conventions and in the battle for the Bill of Rights we can see a radical republican philosophy of more generous proportions. True, the anti-Convention groups often seem a body of naysayers and disingenuous men concerned to preserve their own hold upon local political power. What they feared is not what we fear. And a reading of their speeches may cause us to smile at their parochial views and regret

---

[31] Cecilia Kenyon, "Men of Little Faith: The Anti-Federalists on the Nature of Representative Government," *William and Mary Quarterly*, Vol. 12 (1955), pp. 3-43.

[32] See especially Jackson Turner Main, *The Antifederalists—Critics of the Constitution*, 1781-1788 (Chapel Hill: University of North Carolina Press, 1961); also Robert L. Schuyler, *The Constitution of the United States* (New York: The Macmillan Company, 1923); Vernon Parrington, *Main Currents in American Thought* (New York: Harcourt, Brace and Company, Inc., 1927).

[33] *Records*, Vol. II, pp. 604-50.

their vanished world. The radicals feared central government: especially the powers of the judiciary; the powers to raise an army and a navy;[34] the congressional authority to regulate elections; even the provision empowering Congress to acquire lands for a capital city and for forts and arsenals. The Bill of Rights reveals the same kind of dread of central government. The first ten amendments protect the liberties of individuals, but most of their provisions are directed to the prevention of the accumulation of an irresponsible and tyrannical power. Except for the Bill of Rights, the radical republican philosophy had little direct effect upon the formal Constitution. It was effective principally in compromises made in the dominant approaches. Yet the radicals knew what they would not accept, and into the Constitution they breathed a part of their spirit. For theirs was a philosophy of independence, of a people that wanted a land without a "capital city" culture, without an "Establishment," and without a large standing army. It was also the philosophy of fundamental rights. In that day it was common to call such rights "inalienable." Like the constitutional doctrine of "inalienability" itself—rooted in ancient history and two thousand years of constitutional struggles—the phrase stood for two ideas. "Inalienable rights" meant that such rights belonged to each and to all, that they could not lapse or be taken away. It also meant that such rights were indefeasible: they could not be surrendered. Each man, not only the great, is a keeper of the contract.

---

[34] Gerry wanted to limit the peacetime army to two or three thousand men. Warren, *op. cit.*, p. 483.

Chapter VII

REPUBLIC AND NATION

Politics is marked by contradiction and paradox; and the Federal Convention was no exception. Though the Founding Fathers were tough-minded realists, they were also men of wide-ranging vision. On the one hand, they took as a first premise group and sectional egoism and as an immediate consequent of that premise factiousness and political conflict. On the other hand, they planned boldly, even optimistically, for growing nationhood and for an enlarged conception of American citizenship.

A tension between a narrow, almost cynical realism and a somewhat grandiose idealism did exist in the Convention, as it probably would in any young republic. Many have alleged that the same contradiction has continued to mark American politics,[1] that the Founding Fathers did not plan effectively for their larger vision. Beard would hold that their lofty aspiration was largely pious cant and phrase-mongering, hiding the real motives of economic gain and the protection of property. Others have stressed the underlying negativism in the American Constitution and argued that democracy must be realized *in spite of* the Constitution itself and in the face of the intentions of the Founding Fathers.

---

[1] Cf. Alexis de Tocqueville, *Democracy in America,* Vol. II, Bk. 2; Reinhold Niebuhr, *The Children of Light and The Children of Darkness* (New York: C. Scribners Sons, 1944); and Gabriel A. Almond, *The American People and Foreign Policy* (New York: Harcourt, Brace, and Company, 1950).

Their low view of man and society can be most simply and comprehensively explained by the delegates' general apprehension of the difficulty of establishing a frame of common government in their "disharmonious society." The conditions of eighteenth-century politics may have justified that mood. In any event, those conditions would seem to account for the cautious statesmanship of the delegates; for their separation of national and local democracy; for their careful and conservative grant of powers to the government; and for their stringently applied philosophy of separation of powers and checks and balances.

That cautious statesmanship, however, raises a doubt that the Convention did in fact effectively join specific constitutional prescription with more generous aspirations. It gives point to James Allen Smith's complaint that America is trying to make democratic government work with an undemocratic constitution. Our condition today is not that of the eighteenth century. And most of the specific political characteristics of the delegates' "disharmonious society" no longer obtain. Are the Convention's "republican remedies" for the diseases of popular government appropriate to a twentieth-century democracy? They may, indeed, not only excessively restrain contemporary government but also prevent the populus, the organized political body, from developing and expressing the best spirit of self-government. To attempt a conclusive judgment about these issues would be improper. But we can profitably examine certain themes.

The Constitution was more than the expression of orthodox eighteenth-century republicanism. It was a plan for a nation and an empire as well as for a republic—as that system of government was understood at that time. Also, the Constitution was an effective and coherent synthesis of several philosophies. The synthesis was more than a compromise; the delegates made a distinctive whole that was larger in conception than any of the philosophies or plans that formed the constituent parts. The commerce clause, the national judiciary, and provisions for new territories were elements of the federal solution. They were also the results of sectional compromise. Beyond both of these aspects, however, they were enormously important in the delegates' vision of a future American citizenship. This view demanded and provided for less civic virtue and direct, participatory democracy than would a classical republican model. It may have suited a nation better. However these matters may be, the strategy was effective.

The union of federalism and the representative republic was given concrete expression partly by prohibitions upon the states and even more in the provisions on the powers and organization of Congress, the Presidency, and the Courts. The delegates' handiwork bears throughout the influence of their dual objective: to provide for a republican government and to provide for a future nation. The specific synthesis they made appears especially in the formula for representation in the House and Senate, the role assigned to the Senate, the jurisdiction and powers of the federal judiciary. These provisions also illustrate clearly one fundamental in the political thought of the delegates: their conviction that republican government was an institution that pertained to the whole—to each part of the union and to all of the branches of government taken together.

Representation occupied, for the delegates, much the same place that political parties might in our contemporary thinking. Consequently, the arrangements on representation in the Constitution were the subject of not one but several important bargains or compromises. But the representative balance of the Constitution achieved more than mere balance: the series of compromises worked toward a strengthened, more inclusive, representation for all and each. Multiple constituencies, each resting on a different representative base and principle, insure deliberation and political checks. They also, however, provide access to politics and incentives for action that, within a relatively harmonious polity, afford great political responsiveness. For at least some of the delegates, the term "representative republic" had that meaning too, as well as a narrower republican connotation.

The republic was completed by a Presidency that was "more than a Prime Minister, less than a King." The powers of the Chief Executive were carefully enumerated. The political office was limited. Yet the delegates chose a President instead of a council. He was made accountable to the nation and armed with a formidable prerogative. In creating the office of the Presidency, the delegates preserved a measure of ancient sovereignty—an institution capable for a time, but only for a time, of transcending the representative republic in the name of the common good.

Nevertheless, the Constitution was, in the usual sense of the word, an antipopular institution. The "republican remedies" that were meant to curb and provide alternate channels for the expression of the popular will are a central aspect of the Constitution and express much of its peculiar "genius." The "republican remedies" that figured most prominently in the Convention were, to recapitulate: withdrawal and delegation; fragmentation and filtration; and formal, constitutional, and legal checks on political power. They have, generally, an aura of anti-democracy. What, then, are we to say of these?

A useful way to assess the "republican remedies" is to look at them as the Founding Fathers saw them. To be sure, these devices were intended partly to temper, even to defeat, popular will. They were also, and especially in the eighteenth century, viewed as devices to complete and perfect that will.[2] They were designed to sublimate political conflict

[2] Cf. Martin Diamond, "Democracy and the Federalist: A Reconsideration of the Framers' Intent," *American Political Science Review*, Vol. 53 (1959), pp. 52-68.

and to express the refined product of that conflict through other, more neutral, institutions.

If the republican remedies are considered as devices to sublimate politics, then a further important proposition can be put. To many of the delegates, these checks and constitutional provisions were vital because they made popular republican government possible and tolerable. The point can be made clearer by looking not at the *devices themselves*, but at their *aims*. One aim was to provide for commutative and distributive justice among the states and regions. Another was to preserve an effective balance between the polity and the economy, the public and the private. Madisonian republicanism contributed especially the concept of a wide scope for the judicial temper and the republican elite. And a last aim of the republican remedies was provision for powerful and formal external checks on the exercise of political power.

Certainly the delegates believed that they were hedging cautiously against the future. They were attempting to secure liberty and constitutionalism. But they wanted also to provide for a republic and a nation. And they wanted a maximum of energy in the whole. If their aim was not national democracy, they nevertheless expressed much of the lasting quality of American politics. Perhaps, also, they stated the conditions under which national democracy is possible.

Today, our politics is changed far beyond what the Founding Fathers could have foreseen or comprehended. The interplay of society, the economy, and the polity is complex enough to confound the best of minds. The need to organize and to use collective political power mounts increasingly. The nation and the republic have both far outgrown the simple frame of the eighteenth century. And the Cold War, especially its permanence, adds another dimension to American politics.

The Convention did *not*, as James Wilson lamented, erect a popular pyramid. Nor did it establish either a simple republic or a monarchy. Probably it was best that the delegates stopped where they did. They *did* lay a firm foundation for the conduct of American politics. That end, with all that has been said of their aims, seems to have been their primary intention. To say this is to say also two other things. The Founding Fathers sought a way to establish a continuing enterprise. They also, in their efforts, penetrated to fundamentals. Their principles are not by any description the end of political wisdom about the American polity. They are a good beginning.

The Delegates

Seventy-four delegates were appointed from twelve states (Rhode Island not participating). Of these 74 delegates, 55 went to Philadelphia. Of this latter group of 55, two came very late, five were absent for a major part of the proceedings, and seven left midway or earlier during the sitting of the Convention. Thirty-nine delegates signed the proposed Constitution. Elbridge Gerry, Luther Martin, George Mason, and Edmund Randolph—though active participants in the Convention—refused to sign.

By states, the delegates that attended were:

VIRGINIA
- John Blair
- James Madison
- George Mason
- James McClurg
- Edmund Randolph
- George Washington
- George Wythe

SOUTH CAROLINA
- Pierce Butler
- Charles Pinckney
- Charles Cotesworth Pinckney
- John Rutledge

MARYLAND
- Daniel Carroll
- Luther Martin
- James McHenry
- John Francis Mercer
- Daniel of St. Thomas Jenifer

PENNSYLVANIA
- George Clymer
- Thomas Fitzsimmons
- Benjamin Franklin
- Jared Ingersoll
- Thomas Mifflin
- Gouverneur Morris
- Robert Morris
- James Wilson

MASSACHUSETTS
- Elbridge Gerry
- Nathaniel Gorham
- Rufus King
- Caleb Strong

CONNECTICUT
- Oliver Ellsworth
- William Samuel Johnson
- Roger Sherman

DELAWARE
- Richard Bassett
- Gunning Bedford
- Jacob Broom
- John Dickinson
- George Read

NEW YORK
- Alexander Hamilton
- John Lansing
- Robert Yates

GEORGIA
- Abraham Baldwin
- William Few
- William Houstoun
- William Pierce

NEW JERSEY
- David Brearley
- Jonathan Dayton
- William Churchill Houston
- William Livingston
- William Paterson

NORTH CAROLINA
- William Blount
- Alexander Martin
- William Richardson
- Richard Dobbs Spaight
- Hugh Williamson

NEW HAMPSHIRE
- Nicholas Gilman
- John Langdon

Seventeen of the delegates, mostly from the five states of Virginia, Pennsylvania, Massachusetts, Connecticut, and South Carolina, took the lead in the debates and were especially influential in the framing of the Constitution. Because of the key roles these men played in the Convention, brief accounts of them are given below.

GEORGE WASHINGTON was the most distinguished and revered member of the Convention. He had retired to Mount Vernon and described himself as a Virginia planter, but agreed to participate when he was persuaded that his presence was necessary to the success of the Convention. He was unanimously elected president of the Convention after the withdrawal of Benjamin Franklin. Though Washington spoke little in the course of the debates, partly because of his position as president, he was influential in informal discussion outside the actual meetings. At the time of the Convention, he was fifty-five years old.

JAMES MADISON was thirty-six at the time of the Convention. He was a small man, shy, and described as "always dressed in black." Though a retiring person by nature, he had been active in politics both in Virginia and in Congress, and in the movement for a revision of the Articles. Madison was generally acknowledged to be the most profound scholar and theorist of government in the America of his time. His record of the debates is the principal source of knowledge about the Convention. He was not only important for his theories of government, but also a party to the debate on almost every major provision of the Constitution. Madison's defense of the Constitution in the Virginia ratifying convention is valuable for an understanding of the Constitution.

EDMUND RANDOLPH, thirty-four, the governor of Virginia, was the nominal head of his delegation. The Resolutions that bear his name are thought to be the work of Madison. Randolph spoke little in the Convention and often did not express his thought clearly, but he was an important political figure and carried weight for that reason. He refused to sign the Constitution, pleading his political position as governor of the state of Virginia.

GEORGE MASON, also from Virginia, was sixty-two. He was the author of the Virginia Declaration of Rights, and he was a sturdy champion of popular, especially agrarian, democracy. He refused to sign the Constitution and also opposed it in the Virginia convention, partly because he wanted a Bill of Rights included.

BENJAMIN FRANKLIN of Pennsylvania, at eighty-one, was the oldest member of the Convention. At the time he enjoyed a world reputation both as a philosopher and a statesman. Despite his years he took an active part in the proceedings, depending upon his friend, James Wilson, to read his speeches. Because of his age and perhaps, also, because of his extremely democratic views, the delegates appeared to pay little attention to the specific content of his statements, though several delegates took occasion to extoll him as a great man and to praise his part in soothing ruffled tempers and helping to promote a spirit of healthy compromise.

JAMES WILSON was easily the ablest and most influential member of the Pennsylvania delegation. He was born and educated in Scotland and did not come to America until he was twenty-three. Nevertheless, he was one of the signers of the Declaration of Independence, and had served several times in Congress. He was regarded as one of the ablest lawyers in the United States and later served as a justice of the Supreme Court. Most authorities acknowledge him to have been, next to Madison, the most profound student of government and of political economy in the Convention. In 1787, he was forty-five.

GOUVERNEUR MORRIS, also of Pennsylvania, was thirty-three. A New Yorker by birth, Morris had moved to Pennsylvania when he was defeated for election to Congress in 1779. A lawyer, merchant, and financier, he had been one of the drafters of the New York Constitution of 1777 and had served as Assistant to the Superintendant of Finance (Robert Morris, also of Pennsylvania) under the Confederation. He spoke more than any other member of the Convention and was thought to be brilliant, though some also thought him prejudiced, unprincipled, and impudent.

JOHN RUTLEDGE, forty-eight, was the head of the South Carolina delegation. He had been attorney general and governor of South Carolina as well as a member of Congress. A man of great ability, he was also regarded as the great orator of his day. Rutledge was not prominent in the debates, but was chairman of the Committee of Detail.

CHARLES COTESWORTH PINCKNEY, also of South Carolina, was an Oxford educated planter and a lawyer of great promise. He had risen to be a general during the Revolution and was greatly respected by the Convention delegates. He spoke seldom, but with great conviction and effect.

CHARLES PINCKNEY, ten years younger than his cousin, was at twenty-nine one of the youngest members of the Convention. He was a lawyer and had been a member of Congress. Opinions differ both on his abilities and on his influence. Some hold that his apparent brilliance covered a superficial understanding and that he was slighted by other delegates; others that his views (which favored a strong central government) were important in shaping the final Constitution.

OLIVER ELLSWORTH, forty-two years old, was one of three able delegates from Connecticut. He was a lawyer and had been a member of Congress from Connecticut as well as a judge of the state supreme court. He took an important role in defending the small states and in securing the Connecticut Compromise.

ROGER SHERMAN, the mayor of New Haven, had been a signer of the Declaration of Independence and a member of Congress. At sixty-six, he was, next to Franklin, the oldest member of the Convention. He initially favored a revised Articles rather than a new Constitution, but introduced the Connecticut Compromise when he saw the need for a more radical amendment of the existing system. Like Ellsworth, he was moderate and judicious in his political views, and despite his small-state sympathies, worked ably for the radification of the Constitution.

ELBRIDGE GERRY, forty-three, was prominent in Massachusetts politics and a successful merchant with a deep interest in economic issues. An important figure in the Revolution and in the Congress of the Articles, he was noted for his stern and dogmatic republicanism. Originally, in the Convention, he supported a strong central government, but then opposed it and later the Constitution itself, because they failed to accord with his republican doctrines.

RUFUS KING was a second important delegate from Massachusetts. He supported both a national policy and a strong central government, and worked for ratification in Massachusetts. Later a strong supporter of Hamilton and of Hamilton's doctrines, he became the last Federalist candidate for President in 1819.

ALEXANDER HAMILTON of New York, at thirty, was one of the youngest members of the Convention. Though he did not attend the Convention for its full term and was not, directly, one of the most influential figures there, Hamilton had been an important figure in calling the Convention and in promoting the movement for a strong national government by his work in the New York legislature, in the Continental Congress, and in the Annapolis Convention. With John Jay and James

Madison, Hamilton wrote *The Federalist* to secure ratification of the Constitution in strategically located New York.

JOHN DICKINSON was the most noted member of the Delaware deputation, especially for his early lead in opposition to British rule. He was the author of the "Farmer's Letters," a member of the Continental Congress, and chairman of the committee of Congress that drafted the Articles of Confederation. He had also been president of the executive councils of Delaware and of Pennsylvania. A "small-state" man who later supported the Constitution vigorously, he spoke little in the Convention, but was important in moderating the differences between other groups.

LUTHER MARTIN of Maryland had the distinction of being the most active opponent of the Constitution among the delegates present. He was a lawyer, forty-three years old, and had served as a member of Congress and as attorney-general of Maryland. Allegedly, he was sent by interested parties to Philadelphia expressly to oppose the Constitution, and later attempted to prevent ratification by Maryland. Martin was a frequent and tiresome speaker in the Convention and the delegates appeared to have distrusted him; but he was influential in pressing the "states' rights" point of view.

CONSTITUTION OF THE UNITED STATES

Adopted September 17, 1787. Effective March 4, 1789.

We the people of the United States, in order to form a more perfect union, establish justice, insure domestic tranquillity, provide for the common defense, promote the general welfare, and secure the blessings of liberty to ourselves and our posterity, do ordain and establish this Constitution for the United States of America.

ARTICLE I

SECTION 1. All legislative powers herein granted shall be vested in a Congress of the United States, which shall consist of a Senate and House of Representatives.

SECTION 2. 1. The House of Representatives shall be composed of members chosen every second year by the people of the several States, and the electors in each State shall have the qualifications requisite for electors of the most numerous branch of the State legislature.

2. No person shall be a representative who shall not have attained to the age of twenty-five years, and been seven years a citizen of the United States, and who shall not, when elected, be an inhabitant of that State in which he shall be chosen.

3. Representatives and direct taxes[1] shall be apportioned among the several States which may be included within this Union, according to their respective numbers, which shall be determined by adding to the whole number of free persons, including those bound to service for a term of years, and excluding Indians not taxed, *three fifths of all other persons.*[2] The actual enumeration shall be made within three years after the first meeting of the Congress of the United States, and within every subsequent term of ten years, in such manner as they shall by law direct. The number of representatives shall not exceed one for every thirty thousand, but each State shall have at least one representative; and until such enumeration shall be made, the State of New Hampshire shall be entitled to choose three, Massachusetts eight, Rhode Island and Providence Plantations one, Connecticut five, New York six, New Jersey four, Pennsylvania eight, Delaware one, Maryland six, Virginia ten, North Carolina five, South Carolina five, and Georgia three.

4. When vacancies happen in the representation from any State, the executive authority thereof shall issue writs of election to fill such vacancies.

5. The House of Representatives shall choose their speaker and other officers; and shall have the sole power of impeachment.

SECTION 3. 1. The Senate of the United States shall be composed of two senators from each State, *chosen by the legislature thereof,*[1] for six years; and each senator shall have one vote.

2. Immediately after they shall be assembled in consequence of the first election, they shall be divided as equally as may be into three classes. The seats

1 See the 16th Amendment.
2 See the 14th Amendment.

of the senators of the first class shall be vacated at the expiration of the second year, of the second class at the expiration of the fourth year, and of the third class at the expiration of the sixth year, so that one third may be chosen every second year; and if vacancies happen by resignation, or otherwise, during the recess of the legislature of any State, the executive thereof may make temporary appointments until the next meeting of the legislature, which shall then fill such vacancies.[1]

3. No person shall be a senator who shall not have attained to the age of thirty years, and been nine years a citizen of the United States, and who shall not, when elected, be an inhabitant of that State for which he shall be chosen.

4. The Vice President of the United States shall be President of the Senate, but shall have no vote, unless they be equally divided.

5. The Senate shall choose their other officers, and also a president *pro tempore,* in the absence of the Vice President, or when he shall exercise the office of the President of the United States.

6. The Senate shall have the sole power to try all impeachments. When sitting for that purpose, they shall be on oath or affirmation. When the President of the United States is tried, the chief justice shall preside: and no person shall be convicted without the concurrence of two thirds of the members present.

7. Judgment in cases of impeachment shall not extend further than to removal from office, and disqualifications to hold and enjoy any office of honor, trust or profit under the United States: but the party convicted shall nevertheless be liable and subject to indictment, trial, judgment and punishment, according to law.

SECTION 4. 1. The times, places, and manner of holding elections for senators and representatives, shall be prescribed in each State by the legislature thereof; but the Congress may at any time by law make or alter such regulations, except as to the places of choosing senators.

2. The Congress shall assemble at least once in every year, and such meeting shall be on the first Monday in December, unless they shall by law appoint a different day.

SECTION 5. 1. Each House shall be the judge of the elections, returns and qualifications of its own members, and a majority of each shall constitute a quorum to do business; but a smaller number may adjourn from day to day, and may be authorized to compel the attendance of absent members, in such manner, and under such penalties as each House may provide.

2. Each House may determine the rules of its proceedings, punish its members for disorderly behavior, and, with the concurrence of two thirds, expel a member.

3. Each House shall keep a journal of its proceedings, and from time to time publish the same, excepting such parts as may in their judgment require secrecy; and the yeas and nays of the members of either House on any question shall, at the desire of one fifth of those present, be entered on the journal.

4. Neither House, during the session of Congress, shall, without the consent of the other, adjourn for more than three days, nor to any other place than that in which the two Houses shall be sitting.

SECTION. 6. 1. The senators and representatives shall receive a compensation for their services, to be ascertained by law, and paid out of the Treasury of the United States. They shall in all cases, except treason, felony, and breach of the peace, be privileged from arrest during their attendance at the session of their respective Houses, and in going to and returning from the same; and for any speech or debate in either House, they shall not be questioned in any other place.

---

[1] See the 17th Amendment.

2. No senator or representative shall, during the time for which he was elected, be appointed to any civil office under the authority of the United States, which shall have been created, or the emoluments whereof shall have been increased during such time; and no person holding any office under the United States shall be a member of either House during his continuance in office.

Section 7. 1. All bills, for raising revenue shall originate in the House of Representatives; but the Senate may propose or concur with amendments as on other bills.

2. Every bill which shall have passed the House of Representatives and the Senate, shall, before it becomes a law, be presented to the President of the United States; if he approves he shall sign it, but if not he shall return it, with his objections to that House in which it shall have originated, who shall enter the objections at large on their journal, and proceed to reconsider it. If after such reconsideration two thirds of that House shall agree to pass the bill, it shall be sent, together with the objections, to the other House, by which it shall likewise be reconsidered, and if approved by two thirds of that House, it shall become a law. But in all such cases the votes of both Houses shall be determined by yeas and nays, and the names of the persons voting for and against the bill shall be entered on the journal of each House respectively. If any bill shall not be returned by the President within ten days (Sundays excepted) after it shall have been presented to him, the same shall be a law, in like manner as if he had signed it, unless the Congress by their adjournment prevent its return, in which case it shall not be a law.

3. Every order, resolution, or vote to which the concurrence of the Senate and the House of Representatives may be necessary (except on a question of adjournment) shall be presented to the President of the United States; and before the same shall take effect, shall be approved by him, or being disapproved by him, shall be repassed by two thirds of the Senate and House of Representatives, according to the rules and limitations prescribed in the case of a bill.

Section 8. The Congress shall have the power

1. To lay and collect taxes, duties, imposts, and excises, to pay the debts and provide for the common defense and general welfare of the United States; but all duties, imposts, and excises shall be uniform throughout the United States;

2. To borrow money on the credit of the United States;

3. To regulate commerce with foreign nations, and among the several States, and with the Indian tribes;

4. To establish a uniform rule of naturalization, and uniform laws on the subject of bankruptcies throughout the United States;

5. To coin money, regulate the value thereof, and of foreign coin, and fix the standard of weights and measures;

6. To provide for the punishment of counterfeiting the securities and current coin of the United States;

7. To establish post offices and post roads;

8. To promote the progress of science and useful arts, by securing for limited times to authors and inventors the exclusive right to their respective writings and discoveries,

9. To constitute tribunals inferior to the Supreme Court;

10. To define and punish piracies and felonies committed on the high seas, and offenses against the law of nations;

11. To declare war, grant letters of marque and reprisal, and make rules concerning captures on land and water;

12. To raise and support armies, but no appropriation of money to that use shall be for a longer term than two years;

13. To provide and maintain a navy;

14. To make rules for the government and regulation of the land and naval forces;

15. To provide for calling forth the militia to execute the laws of the Union, suppress insurrections and repel invasions;

16. To provide for organizing, arming, and disciplining the militia, and for governing such part of them as may be employed in the service of the United States, reserving to the States respectively, the appointment of the officers, and the authority of training the militia according to the discipline prescribed by Congress;

17. To exercise exclusive legislation in all cases whatsoever, over such district (not exceeding ten miles square) as may, by cession of particular States, and the acceptance of Congress, become the seat of the government of the United States, and to exercise like authority over all places purchased by the consent of the legislature of the State in which the same shall be, for the erection of forts, magazines, arsenals, dockyards, and other needful buildings; and

18. To make all laws which shall be necessary and proper for carrying into execution the foregoing powers, and all other powers vested by this Constitution in the government of the United States, or in any department or officer thereof.

SECTION 9. 1. The migration or importation of such persons as any of the States now existing shall think proper to admit, shall not be prohibited by the Congress prior to the year one thousand eight hundred and eight, but a tax or duty may be imposed on each importation, not exceeding ten dollars for each person.

2. The privilege of the writ of *habeas corpus* shall not be suspended, unless when in cases of rebellion or invasion the public safety may require it.

3. No bill of attainder or *ex post facto* law shall be passed.

4. No capitation, or other direct, tax shall be laid, unless in proportion to the census or enumeration hereinbefore directed to be taken.[1]

5. No tax or duty shall be laid on articles exported from any State.

6. No preference shall be given by any regulation of commerce or revenue to the ports of one State over those of another: nor shall vessels bound to, or from, one State be obliged to enter, clear, or pay duties in another.

7. No money shall be drawn from the treasury, but in consequence of appropriations made by law; and a regular statement and account of the receipts and expenditures of all public money shall be published from time to time.

8. No title of nobility shall be granted by the United States: and no person holding any office of profit or trust under them, shall, without the consent of the Congress, accept of any present, emolument, office, or title, of any kind whatever, from any king, prince, or foreign State.

SECTION 10. 1. No State shall enter into any treaty, alliance, or confederation; grant letters of marque and reprisal; coin money; emit bills of credit; make anything but gold and silver coin a tender in payments of debts; pass any bill of attainder, *ex post facto* law, or law impairing the obligation of contracts, or grant any title of nobility.

2. No State shall, without the consent of the Congress, lay any imposts or duties on imports or exports, except what may be absolutely necessary for executing its inspection laws; and the net produce of all duties and imposts laid by any State on imports or exports, shall be for the use of the treasury of the United States; and all such laws shall be subject to the revision and control of the Congress.

3. No State shall, without the consent of the Congress, lay any duty of tonnage, keep troops, or ships of war in time of peace, enter into any agreement

[1] See the 16th Amendment.

compact with another State, or with a foreign power, or engage in war, unless actually invaded, or in such imminent danger as will not admit of delay.

ARTICLE II

SECTION 1. 1. The executive power shall be vested in a President of the United States of America. He shall hold his office during the term of four years, and, together with the Vice President, chosen for the same term, be elected as follows.

2. Each State shall appoint, in such manner as the legislature thereof may direct, a number of electors, equal to the whole number of senators and representatives to which the State may be entitled in the Congress: but no senator or representative, or person holding an office of trust or profit under the United States, shall be appointed an elector.

The electors shall meet in their respective States, and vote by ballot for two persons, of whom one at least shall not be an inhabitant of the same State with themselves. And they shall make a list of all the persons voted for, and of the number of votes for each; which list they shall sign and certify, and transmit sealed to the seat of the government of the United States, directed to the president of the Senate. The president of the Senate shall, in the presence of the Senate and House of Representatives, open all the certificates, and the votes shall then be counted. The person having the greatest number of votes shall be the President, if such number be a majority of the whole number of electors appointed; and if there be more than one who have such majority, and have an equal number of votes, then the House of Representatives shall immediately choose by ballot one of them for President; and if no person have a majority, then from the five highest on the list the said House shall in like manner choose the President. But in choosing the President, the votes shall be taken by States, the representation from each State having one vote; a quorum for this purpose shall consist of a member or members from two thirds of the States, and a majority of all the States shall be necessary to a choice. In every case, after the choice of the President, the person having the greatest number of votes of the electors shall be the Vice President. But if there should remain two or more who have equal votes, the Senate shall choose from them by ballot the Vice President.[1]

3. The Congress may determine the time of choosing the electors, and the day on which they shall give their votes; which day shall be the same throughout the United States.

4. No person except a natural born citizen, or a citizen of the United States, at the time of the adoption of this Constitution, shall be eligible to the office of President; neither shall any person be eligible to that office who shall not have attained to the age of thirty-five years, and been fourteen years a resident within the United States.

5. In case of the removal of the president from office, or of his death, resignation, or inability to discharge the powers and duties of the said office, the same shall devolve on the Vice President, and the Congress may by law provide for the case of removal, death, resignation, or inability, both of the President and Vice President, declaring what officer shall then act as President, and such officer shall act accordingly, until the disability be removed, or a President shall be elected.

6. The President shall, at stated times, receive for his services a compensation, which shall neither be increased nor diminished during the period for which he shall have been elected, and he shall not receive within that period any other emolument from the United States, or any of them.

1 Superseded by the 12th Amendment.

7. Before he enter on the execution of his office, he shall take the following oath or affirmation:—"I do solemnly swear (or affirm) that I will faithfully execute the office of President of the United States, and will to the best of my ability, preserve, protect and defend the Constitution of the United States."

SECTION 2. 1. The President shall be commander in chief of the army and navy of the United States, and of the militia of the several States, when called into the actual service of the United States; he may require the opinion, in writing, of the principal officer in each of the executive departments, upon any subject relating to the duties of their respective offices, and he shall have power to grant reprieves and pardons for offenses against the United States, except in cases of impeachment.

2. He shall have power, by and with the advice and consent of the Senate, to make treaties, provided two thirds of the senators present concur; and he shall nominate, and by and with the advice and consent of the Senate, shall appoint ambassadors, other public ministers and consuls, judges of the Supreme Court, and all other officers of the United States, whose appointments are not herein otherwise provided for, and which shall be established by law: but the Congress may by law vest the appointment of such inferior officers, as they think proper, in the President alone, in the courts of law, or in the heads of departments.

3. The President shall have power to fill up all vacancies that may happen during the recess of the Senate, by granting commissions which shall expire at the end of their next session.

SECTION 3. He shall from time to time give to the Congress information of the state of the Union, and recommend to their consideration such measures as he shall judge necessary and expedient; he may, on extraordinary occasions, convene both Houses, or either of them, and in case of disagreement between them with respect to the time of adjournment, he may adjourn them to such time as he shall think proper; he shall receive ambassadors and other public ministers; he shall take care that the laws be faithfully executed, and shall commission all the officers of the United States.

SECTION 4. The President, Vice President, and all civil officers of the United States, shall be removed from office on impeachment for, and conviction of, treason, bribery, or other high crimes and misdemeanors.

ARTICLE III

SECTION 1. The judicial power of the United States shall be vested in one Supreme Court, and in such inferior courts as the Congress may from time to time ordain and establish. The judges, both of the Supreme and inferior courts, shall hold their offices during good behavior, and shall, at stated times, receive for their services, a compensation, which shall not be diminished during their continuance in office.

SECTION 2. 1. The judicial power shall extend to all cases, in law and equity, arising under this Constitution, the laws of the United States, and treaties made, or which shall be made, under their authority;—to all cases affecting ambassadors, other public ministers and consuls;—to all cases of admiralty and maritime jurisdiction;—to controversies to which the United States shall be a party;—to controversies between two or more States;—between a State and citizens of another State;[1]—between citizens of different States;—between citizens of the same State claiming lands under grants of different States, and between a State, or the citizens thereof, and foreign States, citizens or subjects.

---

[1] See the 11th Amendment.

2. In all cases affecting ambassadors, other public ministers and consuls, and those in which a State shall be party, the Supreme Court shall have original jurisdiction. In all the other cases before mentioned, the Supreme Court shall have appellate jurisdiction, both as to law and to fact, with such exceptions, and under such regulations as the Congress shall make.

3. The trial of all crimes, except in cases of impeachment, shall be by jury; and such trial shall be held in the State where the said crimes shall have been committed; but when not committed within any State, the trial shall be at such place or places as the Congress may by law have directed.

SECTION 3. 1. Treason against the United States shall consist only in levying war against them, or in adhering to their enemies, giving them aid and comfort. No person shall be convicted of treason unless on the testimony of two witnesses to the same overt act, or on confession in open court.

2. The Congress shall have power to declare the punishment of treason, but no attainder of treason shall work corruption of blood, or forfeiture except during the life of the person attained.

ARTICLE IV

SECTION 1. Full faith and credit shall be given in each State to the public acts, records, and judicial proceedings of every other State. And the Congress may by general laws prescribe the manner in which such acts, records and proceedings shall be proved, and the effect thereof.

SECTION 2. 1. The citizens of each State shall be entitled to all privileges and immunities of citizens in the several States.[1]

2. A person charged in any State with treason, felony, or other crime, who shall flee from justice, and be found in another State, shall on demand of the executive authority of the State from which he fled, be delivered up to be removed to the State having jurisdiction of the crime.

3. No person held to service or labor in one State under the laws thereof, escaping into another, shall, in consequence of any law or regulation therein, be discharged from each service or labor, but shall be delivered up on claim of the party to whom such service or labor may be due.[2]

SECTION 3. 1. New States may be admitted by the Congress into this Union; but no new State shall be formed or erected within the jurisdiction of any other State; nor any State be formed by the junction of two or more States, or parts of States, without the consent of the legislatures of the States concerned as well as of the Congress.

2. The Congress shall have power to dispose of and make all needful rules and regulations respecting the territory or other property belonging to the United States; and nothing in this Constitution shall be so construed as to prejudice any claims of the United States, or of any particular State.

SECTION 4. The United States shall guarantee to every State in this Union a republican form of government, and shall protect each of them against invasion; and on application of the legislature, or of the executive (when the legislature cannot be convened) against domestic violence.

---

[1] See the 14th Amendment, Sec. 1.
[2] See the 13th Amendment.

ARTICLE V

The Congress, whenever two thirds of both Houses shall deem it necessary, shall propose amendments to this Constitution, or, on the application of the legislatures of two thirds of the several States, shall call a convention for proposing amendments, which in either case, shall be valid to all intents and purposes, as part of this Constitution when ratified by the legislatures of three fourths of the several States, or by conventions in three fourths thereof, as the one or the other mode of ratification may be proposed by the Congress; Provided that no amendment which may be made prior to the year one thousand eight hundred and eight shall in any manner affect the first and fourth clauses in the ninth section of the first article; and that no State, without its consent, shall be deprived of its equal suffrage in the Senate.

ARTICLE VI

1. All debts contracted and engagements entered into, before the adoption of this Constitution, shall be as valid against the United States under this Constitution, as under the Confederation.[1]

2. This Constitution, and the laws of the United States which shall be made in pursuance thereof; and all treaties made, or which shall be made, under the authority of the United States, shall be the supreme law of the land: and the Judges in every State shall be bound thereby, anything in the Constitution or laws of any State to the contrary notwithstanding.

3. The senators and representatives before mentioned, and the members of the several State legislatures, and all executive and judicial officers, both of the United States and of the several States, shall be bound by oath or affirmation to support this Constitution; but no religious test shall ever be required as a qualification to any office or public trust under the United States.

ARTICLE VII

The ratification of the conventions of nine States shall be sufficient for the establishment of this Constitution between the States so ratifying the same.

Done in Convention by the unanimous consent of the States present the seventeenth day of September in the year of our Lord one thousand seven hundred and eighty-seven, and of the independence of the United States of America the twelfth. In witness whereof we have hereunto subscribed our names.

[Names omitted]

Articles in addition to, and amendment of, the Constitution of the United States of America, proposed by Congress, and ratified by the legislatures of the several States pursuant to the fifth article of the original Constitution.

---

1 See the 14th Amendment, Sec. 4.

AMENDMENTS

First Ten Amendments passed by Congress Sept. 25, 1789.
Ratified by three-fourths of the States December 15, 1791.

ARTICLE I

Congress shall make no law respecting an establishment of religion, or prohibiting the free exercise thereof; or abridging the freedom of speech, or of the press; or the right of the people peaceably to assemble, and to petition the government for a redress of grievances.

ARTICLE II

A well regulated militia, being necessary to the security of a free State, the right of the people to keep and bear arms, shall not be infringed.

ARTICLE III

No soldier shall, in time of peace be quartered in any house, without the consent of the owner, nor in time of war, but in a manner to be prescribed by law.

ARTICLE IV

The right of the people to be secure in their persons, houses, papers, and effects, against unreasonable searches and seizures, shall not be violated, and no warrants shall issue, but upon probable cause, supported by oath or affirmation, and particularly describing the place to be searched, and the persons or things to be seized.

ARTICLE V

No person shall be held to answer for a capital, or otherwise infamous crime, unless on a presentment or indictment of a grand jury, except in cases arising in the land or naval forces, or in the militia, when in actual service in time of war or public danger; nor shall any person be subject for the same offense to be twice put in jeopardy of life or limb; nor shall be compelled in any criminal case to be a witness against himself, nor be deprived of life, liberty, or property, without due process of law; nor shall private property be taken for public use without just compensation.

ARTICLE VI

In all criminal prosecutions, the accused shall enjoy the right to a speedy and public trial, by an impartial jury of the State and district wherein the crime shall have been committed, which district shall have been previously ascertained by law, and to be informed of the nature and cause of the accusation; to be confronted with the witnesses against him; to have compulsory process for obtaining witnesses in his favor, and to have the assistance of counsel for his defense.

ARTICLE VII

In suits at common law, where the value in controversy shall exceed twenty dollars, the right of trial by jury shall be preserved, and no fact tried by a jury shall be otherwise reëxamined an any court of the United States, than according to the rules of the common law.

ARTICLE VIII

Excessive bail shall not be required, nor excessive fines imposed, nor cruel and unusual punishments inflicted.

ARTICLE IX

The enumeration in the Constitution of certain rights shall not be construed to deny or disparage others retained by the people.

ARTICLE X

The powers not delegated to the United States by the Constitution, nor prohibited by it to the States, are reserved to the States respectively, or to the people.

ARTICLE XI

Passed by Congress March 5, 1794. Ratified January 8, 1798.

The judicial power of the United States shall not be construed to extend to any suit in law or equity, commenced or prosecuted against one of the United States by citizens of another State, or by citizens or subjects of any foreign State.

ARTICLE XII

Passed by Congress December 12, 1803. Ratified September 25, 1804.

The electors shall meet in their respective States, and vote by ballot for President and Vice President, one of whom, at least, shall not be an inhabitant of the same State with themselves; they shall name in their ballots the person voted for as President, and in distinct ballots, the person voted for as Vice President, and they shall make distinct lists of all persons voted for as President and of all persons voted for as Vice President, and of the number of votes for each, which lists they shall sign and certify, and transmit sealed to the seat of the government of the United States, directed to the President of the Senate;—The President of the Senate shall, in the presence of the Senate and House of Representatives, open all the certificates and the votes shall then be counted;—The person having the greatest number of votes for President, shall be the President, if such number be a majority of the whole number of electors appointed; and if no person have such majority, then from the persons having the highest number not exceeding three on the list of those voted for as President, the House of Representatives shall choose immediately, by ballot, the President. But in choosing the President, the votes shall be taken by States, the representation from each State having one vote; a quorum for this purpose shall consist of a member or members from two thirds of the States, and a majority of all the States shall be necessary to a choice. And if the House of Representatives shall not choose a President whenever the right of choice shall devolve upon them, before the fourth day of March next following, then the Vice President shall act as President, as in the case of the death or other constitutional disability of the President. The person having the greatest number of votes as Vice President shall be the Vice President, if such number be a majority of the whole number of electors appointed, and if no person have a majority, then from the two highest numbers on the list, the Senate shall choose the Vice President; a quorum for the purpose shall consist of two thirds of the whole number of Senators, and a majority of the whole number shall be necessary to a choice. But no person constitutionally ineligible to the office of President shall be eligible to that of Vice President of the United States.

ARTICLE XIII

Passed by Congress February 1, 1865. Ratified December 18, 1865.

SECTION 1. Neither slavery nor involuntary servitude, except as punishment for crime whereof the party shall have been duly convicted, shall exist within the United States, or any place subject to their jurisdiction.

SECTION 2. Congress shall have power to enforce this article by appropriate legislation.

ARTICLE XIV

Passed by Congress June 16, 1866. Ratified July 23, 1868.

SECTION 1. All persons born or naturalized in the United States, and subject to the jurisdiction thereof, are citizens of the United States and of the State wherein they reside. No State shall make or enforce any law which shall abridge the privileges or immunities of citizens of the United States; nor shall any State deprive any person of life, liberty, or property, without due process of law; nor deny to any person within its jurisdiction the equal protection of the laws.

SECTION 2. Representatives shall be apportioned among the several States according to their respective numbers, counting the whole number of persons in each State, excluding Indians not taxed. But when the right to vote at any election for the choice of electors for President and Vice President of the United States, representatives in Congress, the executive and judicial officers of a State, or the members of the legislature thereof, is denied to any of the male inhabitants of such State, being twenty-one years of age, and citizens of the United States, or in any way abridged, except for participation in rebellion, or other crime, the basis of representation therein shall be reduced in the proportion which the number of such male citizens shall bear to the whole number of male citizens twenty-one years of age in such State.

SECTION 3. No person shall be a senator or representative in Congress, or elector of President and Vice President, or hold any office, civil or military, under the United States, or under any State, who having previously taken an oath, as a member of Congress, or as an officer of the United States, or as a member of any State legislature, or as an executive or judicial officer of any State, to support the Constitution of the United States, shall have engaged insurrection or rebellion against the same, or given aid or comfort to the enemies thereof. But Congress may by a vote of two thirds of each House, remove such disability.

SECTION 4. The validity of the public debt of the United States, authorized by law, including debts incurred for payment of pensions and bounties for services in suppressing insurrection or rebellion, shall not be questioned. But neither the United States nor any State shall assume or pay any debt or obligation incurred in aid of insurrection or rebellion against the United States, or any claim for the loss or emancipation of any slave; but all such debts, obligations, and claims shall be held illegal and void.

SECTION 5. The Congress shall have power to enforce, by appropriate legislation, the provisions of this article.

ARTICLE XV

Passed by Congress February 27, 1869. Ratified March 30, 1870.

SECTION 1. The right of citizens of the United States to vote shall not be denied or abridged by the United States or by any State on account of race, color, or previous condition of servitude.

SECTION 2. The Congress shall have power to enforce this article by appropriate legislation.

ARTICLE XVI

Passed by Congress July 12, 1909. Ratified February 25, 1913.

The Congress shall have power to lay and collect taxes on incomes, from whatever source derived, without apportionment among the several States, and without regard to any census or enumeration.

ARTICLE XVII

Passed by Congress May 16, 1912. Ratified May 31, 1913.

The Senate of the United States shall be composed of two senators from each state, elected by the people thereof, for six years; and each senator shall have one vote. The electors in each State shall have the qualifications requisite for electors of the most numerous branch of the State legislature.

When vacancies happen in the representation of any State in the Senate, the executive authority of such State shall issue writs of election to fill such vacancies: *Provided,* That the legislature of any State may empower the executive thereof to make temporary appointments until the people fill the vacancies by election as the legislature may direct.

This amendment shall not be so construed as to affect the election or term of any senator chosen before it becomes valid as part of the Constitution.

ARTICLE XVIII

Passed by Congress December 17, 1917. Ratified January 29, 1919.

After one year from the ratification of this article, the manufacture, sale, or transportation of intoxicating liquors within, the importation thereof into, or the exportation thereof from the United States and all territory subject to the jurisdiction thereof for beverage purposes is hereby prohibited.

The Congress and the several States shall have concurrent power to enforce this article by appropriate legislation.

This article shall be inoperative unless it shall have been ratified as an amendment to the Constitution by the legislatures of the several States, as provided in the Constitution, within seven years from the date of the submission hereof to the states by Congress.

ARTICLE XIX

Passed by Congress June 5, 1919. Ratified August 26, 1920.

The right of citizens of the United States to vote shall not be denied or abridged by the United States or by any State on account of sex.

The Congress shall have power by appropriate legislation to enforce the provisions of this article.

ARTICLE XX

Passed by Congress March 3, 1932. Ratified January 23, 1933.

SECTION 1. The terms of the President and Vice President shall end at noon on the 20th day of January, and the terms of Senators and Representatives at noon on the 3d day of January, of the years in which such terms would have ended if this article had not been ratified; and the terms of their successors shall then begin.

SECTION 2. The Congress shall assemble at least once in every year, and such meeting shall begin at noon on the 3d day of January, unless they shall by law appoint a different day.

SECTION 3. If, at the time fixed for the beginning of the term of the President, the President-elect shall have died, the Vice President-elect shall become President. If a President shall not have been chosen before the time fixed for the beginning of his term, or if the President-elect shall have failed to qualify, then the Vice President-elect shall act as President until a President shall have qualified; and the Congress may by law provide for the case wherein neither a President-elect nor a Vice President-elect shall have qualified, declaring who shall then act as President, or the manner in which one who is to act shall be selected, and such person shall act accordingly until a President or Vice President shall have qualified.

SECTION 4. The Congress may by law provide for the case of the death of any of the persons from whom the House of Representatives may choose a President whenever the right of choice shall have devolved upon them, and for the case of the death of any of the persons from whom the Senate may choose a Vice President whenever the right of choice shall have devolved upon them.

SECTION 5. Sections 1 and 2 shall take effect on the 15th day of October following the ratification of this article.

SECTION 6. This article shall be inoperative unless it shall have been ratified as an amendment to the Constitution by the legislatures of three-fourths of the several States within seven years from the date of its submission.

ARTICLE XXI

Passed by Congress February 20, 1933. Ratified December 5, 1933.

SECTION 1. The Eighteenth Article of amendment to the Constitution of the United States is hereby repealed.

SECTION 2. The transportation or importation into any State, Territory, or possession of the United States for delivery or use therein of intoxicating liquors in violation of the laws thereof, is hereby probihited.

SECTION 3. This article shall be inoperative unless it shall have been ratified as an amendment to the Constitution by conventions in the several States, as provided in the Constitution, within seven years from the date of the submission thereof to the States by the Congress.

ARTICLE XXII

Passed by Congress March 12, 1947. Ratified February 26, 1951.

No person shall be elected to the office of the President more than twice, and no person who has held the office of President, or acted as President, for more than two years of a term to which some other person was elected President shall be elected to the office of the President more than once.

But this article shall not apply to any person holding the office of President when this article was proposed by the Congress, and shall not prevent any person who may be holding the office of President, or acting as President, during the term within which this article becomes operative from holding the office of President or acting as President during the remainder of such term.

This article shall be inoperative unless it shall have been ratified as an amendment to the Constitution by the legislatures of three-fourths of the several states within seven years from the date of its submission to the states by the Congress.

ARTICLE XXIII

Passed by Congress June 16, 1960. Ratified March 29, 1961.

SECTION 1. The District constituting the seat of Government of the United States shall appoint in such manner as the Congress may direct:

A number of electors of President and Vice President equal to the whole number of Senators and Representatives in Congress to which the District would be entitled if it were a State, but in no event more than the least populous state; they shall be in addition to those appointed by the states, but shall be considered, for the purpose of the election of President and Vice President, to be electors appointed by a state; and they shall meet in the District and perform such duties as provided by the twelfth article of amendment.

SECTION 2. The Congress shall have power to enforce this article by appropriate legislation.

ARTICLE XXIV

Passed by Congress August 27, 1962. Ratified January 23, 1964.

SECTION 1. The right of citizens of the United States to vote in any primary or other election for President or Vice President, for electors for President or Vice President, or for Senator or Representative in Congress, shall not be denied or abridged by the United States or any State by reason of failure to pay any poll tax or other tax.

SECTION 2. The Congress shall have the power to enforce this article by appropriate legislation.

Bibliography

BOOKS

Oscar T. Barck, Jr., and Hugh T. Lefler, *Colonial America* (New York: The Macmillan Company, 1958). An up-to-date and concise account of colonial institutions.

Charles A. Beard, *An Economic Interpretation of the Constitution* (New York: The Macmillan Company, 1913). The book in which Beard states his thesis with respect to the framing and adoption of the Constitution.

Carl L. Becker, *The Declaration of Independence—A Study in the History of Political Ideas* (New York: Vintage Books, 1958).* Useful especially for the author's discussion of the relation between the political institutions and the political ideas of the time.

Daniel J. Boorstin, *The Genius of American Politics* (Chicago: University of Chicago Press, 1953).*

Lee Benson, *Turner and Beard—American Historical Writing Reconsidered* (Glencoe, Ill.: The Free Press, 1960). Relates Beard and his argument to the Progressive Era.

Robert E. Brown, *Charles Beard and the American Constitution* (Princeton: Princeton University Press, 1956). One of several important books attacking Beard's thesis.

William M. Chambers, *Political Parties in a New Nation—The American Experience 1776-1809* (New York: Oxford University Press, 1963).* A brief account that also includes the results of much recent research.

Edward S. Corwin, *The Constitution and What It Means Today*, 12th rev'd. ed. (Princeton: Princeton University Press, 1958). The Constitution annotated.

* Available in paperback edition.

Edward S. Corwin, *The "Higher Law" Background of American Constitutional Law* (Ithaca: Cornell University Press, 1957).* Especially valuable for an understanding of the political ideas related to the American tradition of judicial review and constitutional rights.

Merle Curti, *The Growth of American Thought*, 2d ed. (New York: Harper and Brothers, 1951). An intellectual history, dealing primarily with social and cultural ideas.

Alfred de Grazia, *Public and Republic* (New York: Alfred A. Knopf, 1951). A useful treatment of representation, especially as this subject applies to the United States.

Alexis de Tocqueville, *Democracy in America*, 2 vols. (New York: Vintage Books, 1956).* Volume I of this classic is especially valuable for its discussion of the relations of American government and American society and culture in the early years.

Jonathan Elliott, ed., *Debates in the Several State Conventions on the Adoption of the Federal Constitution*, 5 vols. 2d. ed. (Philadelphia: J. B. Lippincott Co., 1901). A standard source for the debates in the state ratifying conventions. The Virginia debates are the most interesting and useful. The debates in Massachusetts and New York are also especially informative. The Philadelphia debates include a lengthy statement by James Wilson that is useful for understanding his views.

Max Farrand, *The Framing of the Constitution of the United States* (New Haven: Yale University Press, 1913). A classic treatment.

Max Farrand, ed. *The Records of the Federal Convention of 1787*, 3 vols., (New Haven: Yale University Press, 1923). A collection of notes of the Convention Proceedings taken by Madison and others together with documents and letters relating to the Convention. Probably the most accessible and useful compilation.

John Fiske, *The Critical Period in American History, 1783-1789*. (New York: Houghton Mifflin Co., 1888). The book that was most influential in establishing the "critical era" description of the period under the Articles. Though much of it is bad historiography by contemporary standards, the book remains both interesting and compelling.

Alexander Hamilton, John Jay, and James Madison, *The Federalist* (Washington, D.C.: National Library Foundation, 1937).* Written to support adoption in the state of New York.

Louis Hartz, *The Liberal Tradition in America* (New York: Harcourt, Brace and Co., 1955). An excellent treatment of American political thought that argues the importance, for America, of John Locke's variety of liberalism.

Richard Hofstadter, *The American Political Tradition* (New York: Alfred A. Knopf, 1948).* A series of interpretive essays. The second essay, entitled "The Founding Fathers: An Age of Realism," is pertinent to the subject of this book.

J. Franklin Jameson, *The American Revolution Considered as a Social Movement* (Boston: Beacon Press, 1956).* The title is self-explanatory. The book is valuable because it discusses the extent to which the Revolution itself either initiated or accelerated social and political change.

Merrill Jensen, *The New Nation—A History of the United States During the*

Confederation—1781-1789 (New York: Alfred A. Knopf, 1950). An important contribution to the reassessment of the period under the Articles.

Earl Latham, ed., *The Declaration of Independence and the Constitution* (Boston: D. C. Heath and Co., 1956).* A useful collection of sources relating primarily to the issue of the Framers' intentions.

Jackson Turner Main, *The Antifederalists—Critics of the Constitution, 1781-1788.* (Chapel Hill: University of North Carolina Press, 1961). Defends the Antifederalists and also includes much valuable detail on the politics of the period.

Forrest McDonald, *We the People—The Economic Origins of the Constitution* (Chicago: Chicago University Press, 1958). Contains valuable material on the political alignments and group affiliations among the pro- and anti-Constitution factions.

Andrew C. McLaughlin, *The Confederation and the Constitution* (New York and London: Harper and Brothers, 1905). A historical account of the period preceding the Convention by an important scholar of American constitutional history.

———, *A Constitutional History of the United States* (New York: D. Appleton-Century Co., Inc., 1935). A classic treatment that discusses especially the relation of the Imperial System, the states, and the Constitution.

Curtis P. Nettels, *The Roots of American Civilization* (New York: F. S. Crofts and Co., 1946). Both interesting and scholarly. Still one of the best general texts on colonial America.

Vernon Parrington, *Main Currents in American Thought* (New York: Harcourt, Brace and Co., 1927). A treatment of political and social thought that also supported and amplified the "Beard thesis."

Roscoe Pound, *The Spirit of the Common Law* (Boston: Marshall Jones Co., 1921).* A good description of the role of the common law in early American society.

Clinton Rossiter, *Seedtime of the Republic—The Origin of the American Tradition of Political Liberty* (New York: Harcourt, Brace and Co., 1953). Treats the political ideas of early America. The book does not go beyond 1780.

J. Allen Smith, *The Spirit of American Government* (New York: Macmillan, 1807). An early, influential attack upon the Constitution and the Convention for their allegedly anti-democratic spirit.

Carl van Doren, *The Great Rehearsal* (New York: The Viking Press, 1948). A popularized account of the Federal Convention.

Charles Warren, *The Making of the Constitution* (Boston: Little, Brown and Co., 1928). The best historical account of the framing of the Constitution.

ARTICLES

Martin Diamond, "Democracy and the Federalist: A Reconsideration of the Framers' Intent," *American Political Science Review,* Vol. 53 (1959), pp. 52-68. A valuable and judicious discussion.

Stanley Elkins and Eric McKitrick, "The Founding Fathers—Young Men of the Revolution," *Political Science Quarterly,* Vol. 76 (1961), pp. 181-218.

An interpretation of the Founding Fathers as youthful and enterprising national leaders.

J. Franklin Jameson, "Studies in the History of the Federal Convention of 1787," *Annual Reports of the American Historical Association,* Vol. 1 (1902). A valuable discussion of some of the documentary sources of knowledge about the Convention.

Cecilia M. Kenyon, "Men of Little Faith: The Anti-Federalists on the Nature of Representative Government," *William and Mary Quarterly,* Vol. 12 (1955), pp. 3-43. A re-assessment of the Antifederalists that is especially useful to the student of political ideas.

John P. Roche, "The Founding Fathers: A Reform Caucus in Action," *American Political Science Review,* Vol. 55 (1961), pp. 799-816. A restatement of the thesis that the Founding Fathers were primarily practical politicians.

Frederick B. Tolles, "The American Revolution Considered as a Social Movement: A Re-Evaluation," American Historical Review, Vol. 55 (1954), pp. 1-12. A review article that discusses the problems in describing the American Revolution as revolutionary.

Index